INTRODUCING REDEMPTION IN CHRISTIAN FEMINISM

INTRODUCING

REDEMPTION
IN CHRISTIAN
FEMINISM

Rosemary R. Ruether

INTRODUCTIONS IN
FEMINIST THEOLOGY

EDITORIAL COMMITTEE

Mary Grey • Lisa Isherwood

Catherine Norris • Janet Wootton

The Pilgrim Press

Cleveland, Ohio

This book is dedicated to my colleagues in

feminist theology around the world,

especially to Ivone Gebara,

who has risked much to speak the truth

The Pilgrim Press, Cleveland, Ohio 44115

© 1998 by Sheffield Academic Press

Originally published by Sheffield Academic Press, Ltd., Sheffield, England

The Pilgrim Press edition published 2000. All rights reserved

Printed in the United States of America on acid-free paper

05 04 03 02 01 00   5 4 3 2 1

ISBN 0-8298-1382-9

Contents

Foreword

Mary Grey

It is a pleasure to introduce the second book in the *Introducing Feminist Theology* series[1] and especially pleasing that this is written by Rosemary Radford Ruether. This book is both a succinct and challenging intro-duction to the central Christian concept of redemption from a Christian feminist perspective, and at the same time engages with the ongoing creativity of Rosemary Ruether's thought. Students of Christian femi-nist theology will find helpful the way she traces the historical develop-ment of the interpretation of Christ as Saviour as either liberating or oppressive for women: even if the dominant effect was oppressive Ruether finds traces of more liberating strands in prophetic sects or, for example, in the neglected contribution of the writing of Hildegard of Bingen.

Writing on redemption is not a simple task.[2] Redemption is more like a cluster of concepts, involving what we mean by salvation, sin and grace, the saviour figure and what exactly happened in the 'Christ event': in Christian feminist terms all of these need to be put under scrutiny as to their effect on women. Already in her earlier work, *Sexism and God-Talk*,[3] Ruether had suggested that whatever contributed to the full becoming of women should be considered as redemptive.[4] In this new work, we find her bringing new voices to the conversation, espe-cially voices of feminist liberation theologians from Asia, Latin America, Africa and women of color in the United States. Redemption is clearly

1. The first was Isherwood and McEwan, (1993).
2. As I found when writing Grey (1989).
3. Ruether 1983.
4. Ruether 1983: 18-19.

conceptualized on a global perspective as the path of liberation transforming both people and oppressive social systems. Redemption also includes the integration of human process with the dying and regeneration of the earth itself. It means learning to celebrate life while acknowledging our fragility and the limits of our life-cycles.

In this new work Rosemary Ruether has made it abundantly clear— yet again—why, for the last twenty years, her work has formed one of the pillars of feminist theology and is again guiding us forward in terms of dialogue, pluralism and a firm rooting in the commitment to end the suffering and oppression of women.

Editor's Preface

BISFT is delighted to be working with SAP in the development of an *Introductions* series. The first book, *Introducing Feminist Theology* (Sheffield: Sheffield Academic Press, 1993) was well-received and provided a solid resource at an academic level for those new to the subject. It also sparked off the idea for a series that would give a taste of the diversity and richness of feminist theology in its global contexts.

BISFT is committed to providing various platforms for feminist theology. These include summer schools, academic courses, monographs and the *Journal of Feminist Theology*. This series is yet another strand in the web. The series will make key ideas and leading voices in feminist theology globally accessible to a wide audience and in this way further the debates. Themes included cover a substantial range of material and a diversity of opinions. The authors have aimed to provide a challenge as well as a solid base for further investigation. Most of all they provide different voices and liberating alternatives to patriarchal theology. They provide transforming options and, we hope, they enable different choices.

We hope you experience both enjoyment and empowerment from this new undertaking.

The Editors

Acknowledgments

I wish to thank the Religion Department of the University of Bristol, England, where I delivered the first three of these chapters as the Benjamin Meeker Visiting Scholar. I also thank the Union Theological Seminary of Richmond, Virginia, where the first four chapters were given as the 1998 Sprunt Lectures.

Introduction

Christianity from its beginning has appeared to offer a gender-inclusive promise of redemption through the death and resurrection of Christ. Christianity gave both women and men the same initiation rite in baptism. Both women and men died to the 'old Adam' in the waters of baptism and rose to newness of life in Christ. The theological claim, itself originally a baptismal formula, found in Paul's letter to the Galatians, that 'in Christ there is no more male and female' appears to offer a neutralization of gender differences in the new humanity in Christ.

Yet male androcentric perspectives biased this inclusive offer of redemption even in the New Testament. The assumption that God was male threw in question women's capacity to be 'in the image of God'. Likewise the maleness of Jesus was read as re-enforcing the view that maleness was necessary for normative humanity. Women could become Christlike only through a symbolic sex change that made them 'spiritually male'.

Views of femaleness as lacking normative and full humanity, as more prone to sin, as more culpable for having caused sin to enter the world in the first place, and has having been created by God to be subordinate skewed the message of equal redemption in Christ. By the second generation of the Christian movement, in writings such as 1 Timothy, women were being defined as those who had been created second and sinned first. They are to keep silent, accept their subordination to the male and bear children in order to be 'saved'. If, from a feminist perspective, such inferiorization of women is itself an expression of sin, then women are not only not saved from sin by Christ, but indeed such Christian definitions re-enforce the sinful condition of violence against them.

This introductory book on feminist perspectives on redemption is divided into two sections. In the first four chapters I survey the historical development of conflicting paradigms of gender and redemption. In Chapter 1 I show the roots of this conflicting paradigm in the New Testament itself. The New Testament shows two important shifts in the definition of redemption: from a this-worldly social definition to an individualistic other worldly definition and from an egalitarian definition that overcomes gender (ethnic and class) discrimination to one that re-enforces gender and class hierarchy in the church, the family and society, while promising a neutralizing of these distinctions in 'heaven'.

By the end of the New Testament period, the second view, which was other worldly and re-enforced gender hierarchy in church and society had triumphed in the dominant leadership of the church. Groups that maintained the egalitarian vision of redemption continued in the second century, but they were being marginalized by the emerging dominant church and defined as 'heretical'.

Moreover the egalitarian perspective found in gnostic and apocalyptic movements themselves accepted a view that gender hierarchy was the normative 'order of creation'. They differed from the dominant orthodoxy only in seeing this creation itself as transient or even as having been created by evil, fallen powers. Thus they saw this hierarchy as already dissolved here and now for the baptized Christian living 'in Christ'.

In Chapter 2 I trace the conflict and mingling of these two paradigms from second-century Christianity to the end of the Middle Ages. The Latin Church Father Augustine used the view of women as created subordinate even before the Fall and more guilty in sin to suppress the residual views that baptism dissolved gender subordination in the church here and now. Augustine thought that women would be spiritually equal in heaven according to their merits, but would get there only by accepting their subordination here on earth, both as wives and as celibates.

This Augustininan view was re-enforced by Thomas Aquinas, who adopted the Aristotelian view that women's inferiority is not simply the result of divine law, but resides in their biological defectiveness. Yet the alternative view that celibacy and the vocation to the spiritual life overcomes gender subordination lingered, particularly in female monasticism. Leading female mystics from the twelfth to the fifteenth centuries also introduced sophiological images of God and Christ. By bringing the female Wisdom symbol into the definition of God and Christ, women mystics, such as Hildegard of Bingen and Julian of Norwich, began to undermine the androcentric theology that made women incapable of being theomorphic and Christomorphic.

The Reformation saw both the patriarchal and the egalitarian paradigms of redemption emerge with new clarity and force. Luther and Calvin reaffirmed the patriarchal paradigm with a new emphasis on marriage as the normative life style for all Christians. By dismissing celibacy and monastic life, the Magisterial reformers eliminated alternative vocations to subordinate wifehood for women and lingering notions that women rose from subordination to equality through celibacy.

But alternative reform movements, in the humanist and radical reformation traditions, particularly the Quakers, rediscovered and developed the New Testament egalitarian paradigm of redemption. They claimed an egalitarian view of the original creation in the light of which gender subordination was defined as an expression of sin and the Fall, not as the will of God. Redemption in Christ was then defined as restoring this original equality in the image of God for women equally with men. The classical Christian theology of subordination was seen as a betrayal of the good news of redemption in Christ for women equally with men.

Nineteenth-century Americans saw two egalitarian paradigms of gender and redemption meet and mingle. In the Shakers medieval views that God is female and male (Wisdom and Power), and that women and men overcome subordination and enter into equality through celibacy were continued. The Shakers added the new proclamation of the appearance of a female Christ, representing the female side of God and completing the redemption left incomplete in the male Christ.

In feminist abolitionist leaders, such as the Grimké sisters and Lucretia Mott, the Quaker theology of original and restored equality was merged with the liberal political theory that 'all men are created equal', to found a struggle for women's full equality in both church and society as the true meaning of redemption.

In the twentieth century this claim of original and restored equality of the genders has blossomed into increasingly diverse and global movements of feminist theology in North America, Western Europe, Latin America, Asia and Africa. Feminist theologians around the world are contextualizing the feminist understanding of original and renewed equality to struggle for a redemptive transformation of their societies. Here it is assumed that redemption means overcoming patriarchal subordination of women in all its forms and creating societies and cultures of just and loving mutuality between men and women across classes and races.

Having surveyed this historical development in Christian theology, the second half of the book focuses on four key theological themes. In Chapter 5 I discuss the meaning of conversion and transformation, sin and grace, from the perspective of feminist theology. In Chapter 6 I focus on the problem of an androcentric, patriarchal definition of Christ as representative of a male God and a view that only the male possesses full and normative humanness. I ask whether the definition of Christ as 'fully God' and 'fully man' can be liberated from these androcentric definitions of divinity and humanity to become fully inclusive of women as those who are both saved by Christ and able to 'image' Christ.

In Chapter 7 the questions of the cross and atonement are addressed. Have the classical definitions of atonement through the blood of the cross resulted in the perpetuation of the cycle of violence for women, rather than overcoming it? Have women been both scape-goated by the cross and made to bear it disproportionately as their way of atoning for the sin of Eve? In this chapter I discuss several significant feminist challenges to the view that the suffering of Christ on the cross is redemptive and a model for Christian redemptive life.

Finally, in Chapter 8, I ask what can we hope for in redemption? Do we expect that society will be transformed into increasingly just and loving social relations, overcoming patriarchal hierarchies? Do we hope that God will intervene to destroy all evil and bring about a transformed earth where 'every tear is wiped away'? Or do we hope simply to doff the body at death, assured of eternal happiness in heaven as souls liberated from the mortal body? In this concluding chapter, these various views of the ultimate meaning of redemption for future hope and eschatology are examined and alternative visions proposed from a feminist perspective.

Chapter One

In Christ No More Male and Female?
Conflicting Paradigms of Redemption and Gender in Scripture

Redemption in Hebrew Scripture and Early Judaism

In Hebrew Scripture redemption originally had a very concrete social meaning. It referred to the ransoming of a slave from bondage. In a world where slave labor was assumed and persons became enslaved in a variety of ways, from kidnapping and capture in war to being sold by their families or even selling themselves to pay debts, ransoming from slavery generally meant a monetary transaction. Money was paid by an advocate, even by the slave him or herself, to the slave-owner to buy the slave's freedom.

But this common social transaction was translated into collective and religious meanings in the course of Israel's history. It came to refer to national redemption from slavery in Egypt effected by divine intervention. God's deliverance of Israel from Egyptian bondage became the paradigmatic story of redemption of the people as a whole. It also acquired psycho-spiritual dimensions: bondage to sin, disease and demonic possession. Such deliverances could be related to the cultic context: expiation from sin was effected through temple sacrifice. The idea of expiation through blood sacrifice later became associated with martyrdom. An especially holy teacher or prophet who was martyred could be seen as making expiation for sin for the nation as a whole.

Redemption developed eschatological dimensions. In later prophetic and apocalyptic literature Israel was seen as awaiting deliverance in a future historical time from bondage to foreign empires, seen as manifestations of cosmic evil powers. Gradually this was translated into cosmological terms: the whole creation awaits deliverance from evil and a transformation into a new age when injustice and finally mortality itself is overcome. This work of deliverance could be seen as embodied in a mediator, a great warrior/king who represented both God and the people Israel in the work of redemption.[1]

These developments of the idea of redemption in Hebrew Scripture and early Judaism did not explicitly speak of gender, but an ethnocentric and patriarchal framework was usually taken for granted. That is, the subject of redemption was seen as Israel as a nation, liberated from bondage to other nations, and the new age to come was one of national vindication and flourishing in a society of male leaders and male householders. But the ethnic and patriarchal limits of this vision began to be pressed in some movements of inter-testamental Judaism. More universalist prophetic movements saw all nations delivered from evil, by submitting themselves to Israel's God.

The Hellenistic Jewish philosopher Philo, describes an ideal Jewish contemplative community, which he called the Therapeutae, those who practice a way of life of physical and spiritual healing. In this sect women as well as men study Torah during the week and celebrate their redemption on the sabbath. The distinctions between men and women are overcome through sexual renunciation and adoption of the spiritual life. Also, slavery is identified with an unjust social order contrary to nature, rejected by the 'healed ones'. Philo sees inequality between persons as the 'cause of all evil'. In his words:

> They do not use the ministration of slaves, looking upon the possession of servants or slaves to be a thing absolutely and wholly contrary to nature, for nature has made all humans free, but injustice and covetousness of some men who prefer inequality, that cause of all evil, having subdued some, has given to the more powerful authority over those who are weaker.[2]

This rich and complex development of ideas of redemption was inherited by the early Christian movement. Different strands in these traditions, national or universal, cultic or spiritual, patriarchal or egalitarian, overcoming gender and class hierarchy, would be sources of contention among early Christians. Jesus himself was the decisive reinterpreter of these traditions about redemption. His teachings and practice, and his death, laid the basis for early Christian understandings of him as the expiating martyr and coming messiah. But that still left room for

1.   For an overview of the idea of redemption in Hebrew Scripture, see Schüssler Fiorenza (1987: 836-38).
2.   Philo, 'The Therapeutae', in Glatzer 1971: 326.

many differences of view, particularly on issues of gender, slavery and nationalism, and the relation of inward and outward, present and future aspects of change. How inclusive and how imminent were the transformations effected by redemption?

This chapter will focus particularly on how change in gender status was connected with redemption in New Testament Christianity. Let me begin by a brief discussion of Jesus' own ministry, which I believe laid the basis for gender status in the early Church. I follow New Testament scholar Dominic Crossan in believing that the distinctive characteristic of Jesus' preaching and practice lay in a conviction that the long-awaited coming of the Kingdom of God, the redemption of Israel, was already beginning in incipient form, and could be experienced here and now in signs of the Kingdom. These signs of the Kingdom were expressed in healing and exorcisms, the breaking of the power of Satan over the lives of sick and possessed people and in celebratory table fellowship in which the former divisions between pure and impure, the righteous, with their careful rituals of purity, and the unwashed and polluted, who have no access to such status, were broken down.[3]

This overcoming of divisions included Jews and other groups, such as Canaanites and Samaritans, and also male and female. Early Christians experienced themselves as a new kind of family where such divisions had been overcome, where those who previously had little hope for God's favor had been gathered into a new community of God's beloved children. This belief was expressed in certain iconoclastic reversals of prevalent gender and social status; good news to the poor, those now most despised, poor widows, women diseased and bent over, polluted by bodily fluxes, are likely to be more in tune with God and God's prophet than the official religious leaders, where 'the tax collectors and prostitutes will go into the Kingdom of God ahead of You, the High Priests, Elders of the People and Pharisees'.[4]

When this compelling healer and prophet was snatched away from his followers and subjected to the terrible death of an enemy of the Roman state, crucifixion, his followers initially scattered in dismay. But they soon reassembled, convinced that he had not been defeated by death, but had risen, was still among them in Spirit, and would soon return to

3.   Crossan 1991.
4.   Lk. 4.18-19, reflecting Isa. 61.1-2; 58.6. For other examples of such iconoclastic egalitarianism and concern for women, see Mk 5.25-34 (Mt. 9.20); Mk 7.24-30 (Mt. 15.21-28); Lk. 13.10-17; and Mt. 21.31.

inaugurate God's reign. Meanwhile they should continue to preach the good news in his name and to baptize.

It is likely that some of Jesus' female followers, led by Mary Magdalene, played a key role in this conviction of Jesus' resurrection and its announcement to the male disciples who had fled. This is evidenced by the appearance in all four Gospels of a story line in which a group of women disciples are the faithful remnant at the cross and the first witnesses of the resurrection.[5] Women were also seen as included in that outpouring of the Spirit at Pentecost in which 'your sons and daughters will prophesy', empowering his followers, both men and women, to go out to preach, testifying to the good news in the name of their risen Lord.[6]

As the Jesus movement spread to major cities of the Diaspora, such as Antioch and Alexandria, first as a religious group within Judaism and then beginning to differentiate itself as a religious movement of Jews and Gentiles, women continued to play important roles as providers of houses and resources for table fellowship, as members of missionary teams and as local leaders, teachers and prophets.[7] These roles of women reflected both the gender inclusive community around Jesus, justified by its Kingdom theology, and also some changed economic patterns in the first century that allowed new classes of women (and men) from freedmen and diverse ethnic origins to play roles in small manufacturing and trade in a united Roman empire.[8]

These experiences of women among early Christian leaders suggested to some early Christian interpreters a baptismal theology in which incorporation into the new redeemed humanity in Christ, anticipating the coming of the Kingdom, was understood as breaking down the traditional hierarchy of male and female. I suggest that the gender form of this formula probably came first, since it exists in various forms independent of the additional components of 'Jew and Greek, slave and free'. There are various non-canonical early Christian texts where we

---

5.   Mt. 28.1-10; Mk 16.1-8; Lk. 25.1-11; Jn 20.1-18. It has been common among New Testament stories to regard the 'empty tomb' stories as late, and thus to discredit the importance of the women as first witnesses of the resurrection. But the fact that all four Gospels depict the women as the first witnesses indicates that this was well established in the tradition from which the empty tomb story came.

6.   Acts 2.17-18.

7.   See Schüssler Fiorenza 1983: esp. 160-98.

8.   See Pomeroy 1975: 149-63, 198-202; also Pomeroy 1984.

find only the gender version of this formula, such as the Gospel of the Egyptians, where Jesus replies to Salome's query about when redemption will happen by saying, 'When you tread on the garment of shame, and when the two become one, the male with the female, neither male nor female.'

A Corinthian sermon from the early second century quotes a similar saying of Jesus: 'For the Lord himself when asked by someone when his Kingdom will come, said, "When the two are one, and the outside as the inside, and the male with the female neither male nor female."' The Gospel of Thomas has a similar view of Jesus' teaching: 'Jesus said to them, when you make the two one, and the outside as the inside, and the above as the below, and you make the male with the female into a single one, so that the male shall not be male and the female not be female... then shall you enter the Kingdom.'[9]

I also concur with other scholars in suggesting an Alexandrian origin for this idea, rooted in the Hellenistic Jewish theology of Philo. Philo developed a theological anthropology in which humanity was created by God in God's image first in a spiritual non-gendered form. Only later, as a result of a sinful fall from original unity, did division into male and female arise. For Philo the division into male and female did not belong to the original creation, but to a later fall.[10] As we have seen, Philo also extolled a Jewish monastic community of celibate women and men, the Therapeutae, which he saw as recovering their original spiritual unity by renouncing sexual relations.

If this view of the link to Philo is correct, the Christians that formulated the baptismal formula that in Christ there is no more male and female saw themselves within this world view of an original spiritual unity of male and female restored. They interpreted the inclusion of women in early Christian leadership and community in terms of a new redemptive identity in which the sexual dimorphism of sinful fallenness had been overcome. The redeemed humanity given to them in Christ through baptism restored them to their non-gendered original unity and communion with God.

Does this mean there was a clearly established theology and practice

9. See Cameron 1982: 52; *1–2 Clem.* 12.2-6 and the *Gos. Thom.* 22.4-7 in Miller (1994: 309). For discussion on the relation of these texts to the Gal. 3.28, see MacDonald (1987: 17-63).

10. Philo, 'On the Creation of the World', 47-53. For discussion see MacDonald (1987: 26-30).

of gender equality in the earliest Christianity? I am not arguing that there was such a 'discipleship of equals', as has been claimed by some New Testament scholars, most notably Elizabeth Schüssler Fiorenza, in the sense of a programmatic theory and general practice accepted by all for the first generation.[11] Rather we should probably think more in terms of an *ad hoc* situation here and there in which some women, generally from life situations where they had some economic means to live independently, were able to participate in teams of traveling evangelists, host local Christian fellowships and engage in leadership in catechesis and prophetic prayer in Christian churches. But the baptismal theology that some Christians created and used to justify these practices, as well as the practices themselves, were soon contested by other Christian leaders. The center of this conflict occurred in Pauline communities both in Paul's lifetime and after his death.

Redemption and Gender in Conflict in Corinth

In my view Paul himself originated neither the baptismal theology of overcoming gender dimorphism (no more male and female), and also did not add the religio-ethnic and class pairs to this baptismal theology (no more Jew or Greek, no more slave and free). This addition was probably also pre-Pauline, but in the context of a Hellenistic Jewish-Christian mission that Paul joined, one that combined membership of slaves, freed men and women, Jews and Greeks, and had women among its leaders. This triadic formula suggested a reversal of the patterns of social discrimination in both Jewish and Greek cultures, which prized the superiority of one's ethnicity, Jew or Greek, as well as maleness and free status, at the expense of women, slaves and other ethnic groups. This is found in Greek philosophical formulas in which a man thanks the gods that he was born Greek and not barbarian, male and not female, free and not slave, and Jewish religious formulas where a man thanks God that he was born Jew and not Greek, male and not female, free and not slave.[12]

The claim of some Christians that in Christ these divisions are overcome suggests not only a belief that the cosmic fall is spiritually over-

11. See, particularly, Schüssler Fiorenza 1983: 140-51.

12. The Hellenistic thanksgiving is attributed to Thales: Diogenes Laertius, *Lives of the Philosophers* 1.33, to the Plato, Lactantius, *Divine Institutes*, 3.19. For the Hebrew version of the prayer, see MacDonald (1987: 122-23).

come, but also a new oneness in Christ that has potentially upsetting social consequences for life in the Christian community. Women as well as men, Gentiles and Jews, slaves and freed people all share the same table fellowship, all may speak in prayer and prophesy, teach, evangelize on a somewhat equal basis. The male-female part of this formula had originally suggested an ontological change in which baptismal regeneration restored men and women to a pre-fallen spiritual wholeness before sexual dimorphism. For Philo this was expressed sexually in celibacy, socially by retirement to a monastic community. But this was not the social setting of early Christians that used this formula, where married, single and widows/widowers, slaves and people of diverse ethnicities mingled together in the midst of ordinary work lives. So how would such an understanding of the relations between these various people be understood in the midst of ordinary lives where the social power of the paterfamilias over wives, children and slaves was taken for granted in the larger society?

Paul probably did not create this baptismal formula in either its single paired or triadic form, because he did not promote the idea of an ontological change of return to pre-fallen wholeness already available now or the implications of social equality of women with men, slave with masters that would allow either women or slaves to throw off their subordination to the paterfamilias of the household. Paul used it in Gal. 3.28 because he had accepted this formula from the tradition he joined, but he had not yet focused on the ontological and social implications of this theology, especially for gender relations. The part of the formula that interested him primarily in Galatians was the Jew–Greek ethno-religious pair, or as he puts it, 'In Christ neither circumcision or uncircumcision counts for anything, but only faith working in love' (Gal. 5.6).

Only when Paul entered into a conflict with parties in the Christian churches in Corinth that endorsed the gender aspect of this formula, in both its ontic and social implications, did he feel the need to clarify his own views and differentiate them from those of these Corinthians. In the process he reformulated the Christian theology of redemption in such a way that it lost both its ontic gender implications and also its social implications both for women and for slaves in patriarchal households.

Corinth in 50 CE was a booming center of commerce where Italians, Greeks and Orientals, including Jews, mingled. Paul was not the only Christian evangelist working there. Apollos, a Jewish-Christian originally from Alexandria, a disciple of the followers of John the Baptist, who had been further instructed by the missionary couple, Priscilla and Aquila in Ephesus, also arrived while Paul was there.[13] Paul left Corinth in 51 CE for Ephesus. In 54 CE he wrote a letter to the Corinthians to re-establish his authority there, which he saw as being challenged, and to refute many ideas and practices that he saw as dangerous. The church at Corinth had a number of strong female leaders, some of whom we know by name as supporters of Paul, such as Priscilla, Chloe, who hosted a church in her house, and Phoebe, leader of the church in the port city of Corinth, Cenchreae.[14] There were others that are unnamed and likely represented factions that Paul opposed.

These Corinthian women and men that Paul argues with seem to have endorsed some version of a realized eschatology in which the power of the demons or fallen angels was already overcome.[15] For them the baptismal new life in Christ means anticipating the Kingdom in which there is no more marrying and giving in marriage. Consequently some were not marrying, or not remarrying if they were widows, or if married were withdrawing from marital relations. Ecstatic possession allowed women as well as men to pray and prophesy in the Spirit, the women discarding the head covering that signaled traditional female subordination.[16]

Paul found these practices, and the theology of realized eschatology that underlay them, highly problematic and set out to change them on a number of issues. In the process he sought to shore up internal status hierarchy of both gender and ministerial class, as well as external boundaries between Christian and pagan, signaled by food and sexual practices. Paul begins by asserting his own apostolic authority, claiming he wishes to overcome factions in the church, particularly between himself and Apollos.

13. Apollos is mentioned in 1 Cor. 3.4-6 and 4.6. Crossan (1991: 298) and MacDonald (1987: 66) see Apollos as having brought the Philonic theology to Corinth.

14. Priscilla is mentioned in Acts 18.2, 18, 26; 1 Cor. 16.19; Rom. 16.3 and 2 Tim. 4.19. The household of Chloe appears in 1 Cor. 1.11 and Phoebe in Rom. 16.1. For discussion of these women see Meeks (1983: 26-27, 57-60, 75, 118). See also Schüssler Fiorenza 1983:171-72.

15. For the development of the Watchers or fallen angels story, see Prusak (1974: 89-116).

16. For the literature that argues various interpretations on head covering, see Wire (1990: 220-23). Also MacDonald 1987: 72-91.

Paul praises the Corinthians for the many spiritual gifts of speech and knowledge they have received from Christ. But he then speaks of his own weakness and sufferings, laying out a theology of the cross in the light of which the Corinthian belief that they possess high wisdom is identified with worldly foolishness of those still infants in the faith, not yet ready for solid food. He thereby cuts the Corinthian opponents down to size as infantile beginners in the faith, not yet possessed of the fullness of redemptive life, knowledge and power, as they believe. He then brandishes his magisterial power over them, as their 'father in the gospel', threatening to 'come to you with a stick' if they fail to heed his admonitions.[17]

Paul then addresses a number of disciplinary issues as exemplifying their mistakes, which they have taken as spiritual wisdom. I will discuss those having particularly to do with sex and gender issues. One of these is the question of not marrying or withdrawal from marital relations. This is a touchy one for Paul, because Paul is himself celibate and espouses a version of the belief that withdrawal from sex anticipates the Kingdom. But he opposes the general adoption of this life style, since he believes that they are not ready for it and they will fall into immorality. Also he recognizes that celibacy for women affirms their belief that they have transcended gender subordination in the household and can act with new freedom. Although Paul's view that each spouse in marriage has authority over the body of the other appears egalitarian to us today, it denied what the women sought to gain by celibacy, namely, authority over their own bodies.

Paul advises that all should marry and maintain sexual relations, even though they might temporarily withdraw for prayer. He also advises the unmarried to marry. Although he acknowledges that the time of final crisis is near when distinctions of women and men, slave and free will disappear, it has not yet arrived. No one should 'jump the gun' by seeking freedom if they are slaves, or withdrawing from marriage if married. Paul seems to have in mind the baptismal theology: 'no more male and female, slave and free', but he is saying this transformation is not yet realized. It will be realized in a future Kingdom that is near but not yet here.[18]

Paul goes on to the matter of women's head coverings, insisting that they cover their heads when praying or prophesying. Although he does

17. 1 Cor. 4.21; see Wire 1990: 43-71.
18. 1 Cor. 7; see discussion in Wire 1990: 73-97.

not deny them the right to pray and prophesy in the Christian assemblies, he justifies head coverings on the basis of a hierarchical theology of orders of creation: God is the head of Christ, Christ head of the male and the male the head of the female. This hierarchical view of creation counteracts what was probably the Corinthians' belief in an original spiritual unity of male and female united in the divine logos, restored through Christ in baptism. For Paul the created cosmic order is hierarchical, God over Christ, male over female, and this cosmic order remains. So women should continue to have 'authority' on their heads, to signify their proper place in this hierarchical cosmology and their secondary status in the image of God.

Denying women's equality in the image of God, Paul claims that men should not cover their heads for they are the image and glory of God, while women have only a secondary reflection of this image of God under the man.[19] Paul also refers to a common view of Jewish teachers of his day, that angels were seduced to fall by the sight of the beautiful hair of women's uncovered heads and this union caused the birth of demonic powers, so women should also cover their heads 'because of the angels'.[20] Contrary to the Corinthians' view, these angelic powers have not yet been conquered.

Paul also rebukes the spontaneous and egalitarian prophetic speech practiced by the Corinthians, insisting that a few should speak, in sequence and with rational interpretation. In a society where women were mostly uneducated and banned from the exercise of public rhetoric, but allowed ecstatic, spirit-possessed speech, this would have had a chilling effect on women's public testimony.[21] However, the statement in 1 Cor. 14.34-36 that 'women should remain silent in the churches, they are not allowed to speak, but must be in submission, even as the Law says' is probably not from Paul, but is a gloss from a later hand.[22]

Paul also lays out an analogy of the Christian community to the body in which different members have different functions. Not all should participate in the same way. There are different functions that should

---

19. 1 Cor. 11.7; see discussion of this text by Fatum (1991: 56-137).

20. See Wire's view on the meaning of the angel reference (Wire 1990: 121-22).

21. 1 Cor. 14; see Wire 1990: 102-12.

22. Wire believes that Paul wrote 1 Cor. 14.34-36 as the culmination of his purpose in this letter, which was to silence the women altogether (Wire 1990: 149-58, 229-31). Other scholars regard it as a gloss that reflects the period of 1 Tim. whose language it echoes. See MacDonald 1983: 87.

not be confused, although all parts are indispensable. The weaker and less honorable members of the body should be honored by covering them. This analogy of the community to a hierarchically ordered body suggests a certain hierarchy of leadership roles that would have had a male clerical effect. By implication women are compared to the sexual parts of the body, which, though indispensable, should be covered. This analogy makes clear how much Paul thinks of women's uncovered heads as sexually provocative, comparable to appearing in public with uncovered 'private parts'.[23] Perhaps the intense conflicts in the Islamic world today over women's head covering can give us today some clue as to the vehement feelings this issue aroused for Paul.

The letter culminates in Paul's theology of redemption. Here he lays out an ordered sequence; first Christ's resurrection, then the apostolic witnesses of the resurrection that culminate in Paul himself, but significantly leaves out the women's witnesses found in all four gospels.[24] Then there will be a third and still future stage in which Christ conquers the demonic powers, then death itself, and then hands over the Kingdom to the Father. Only then will sin and death be conquered, but this is not yet. The Corinthians' theology of realized eschatology is thereby rejected, and with it a view that the hierarchical ordering of male over female, master over slave can be already annulled. This will happen at the end, but this is not yet. For now all must stay in their present social ranks.

Gender and Redemption in Two Types
of Post-Pauline Churches

The reception of Paul's efforts to reimpose his authority and correct the Corinthians' theology and practices probably increased the dissension between factions and anger toward him by those of different views, although later visits and letters attempt to smooth this over. But the divisions represented by parties in the Corinthian church deepened in Pauline churches in the generation after Paul. One line of Pauline tradition moved toward patriarchalization, in which equality in Christ is spiritualized and combined with a mandate for continued social subordination of women and slaves. A second group continued to affirm a theology of redemption in which women's subordination is already

23. See D'Angelo 1995: 131-64.
24. 1 Cor. 15.1-8; see Wire 1990: 161-63.

overcome. This is expressed by the rejection of marriage, departure from the patriarchal household and freedom to engage in itinerant preaching. The one line of patriarchal Paulinism became enshrined in the canonical New Testament, while the other was relegated to the fringes and gradually suppressed.

Patriarchal Paulinism is represented by the letters to the Colossians and Ephesians, as well as 1 Peter.[25] Colossians contains a strong theology of realized eschatology. The baptized have been rescued from the Kingdom of Darkness and transferred to the Kingdom of God's beloved Son, have conquered the demonic powers and have passed from death to immortal life. This has overcome the old divisions of Jew and Greek, slave and free, to which the author adds, Barbarian and Scythian, but omits male and female. But this new equality in Christ is spiritualized and combined with continued subjection to the hierarchical orders of the patriarchal family, in the commands to wives to be subject to their husbands, children to parents and slaves to master. The letter to the Ephesians further Christianizes the patriarchal family, comparing the hierarchical ordering of Christ to the church as head to body, husband to wife. An alternative view that also claims the authority of Paul is found in non-canonical writings, such as the *Acts of Paul and Thecla*. In this writing, Thecla, a young virgin engaged to be married, is converted by Paul and straightaway rejects her husband to be and adopts celibacy. Dressing as a man, she departs from her confinement in the household to travel and preach, pursued by the agents of family and state represented by her mother, her fiancé and the governor. Thrown to lions not once but twice, she emerges triumphant, baptizes herself and is commissioned by a reappeared Paul to return to her home town of Iconium to preach.[26]

It has been speculated that such early Christian texts that exalt women who reject marriage and household to teach publicly reflect a ministry of unmarried or widowed Christian women in the early Churches. They were catechists, carried out the baptismal rites for women and visited the female sick in their homes, functions that demanded a female ministry, since adult baptism took place in the nude and men other than the husband were not allowed in the female quarters of the houses.[27]

25. See discussion of these texts in Schüssler Fiorenza (1983: 251-59, 266-70).

26. The English translation of the *Acts of Paul and Thecla* is in Roberts and Donaldson (1870, XVI, pp. 279-92).

27. See Davies 1980.

The clearest confrontation between these two types of Deutero-Pauline theologies and practices is found in 1 Timothy, a letter attributed to Paul but written in the first half of the second century. In this epistle women are called to submit to their husbands. Women teaching or having authority over men in the church are specifically prohibited. These commands are justified through a theology of Creation and Fall that sets up a doubly enforced hierarchy of men over women: women were created second and sinned first, therefore they are to keep silent in view of both their secondary place in creation and their punished status due to their primacy in sin.[28] It is this text that would decisively shape the gender hierarchy of Christian theology and practice into the twentieth century.

The writer of 1 Timothy connects this continued mandate of female subordination with rejection of celibacy. Not only are the marital ordinances of Genesis still in place, but it is through bearing children that women are to atone for their sin. The gender hierarchy of the patriarchal family also is the model for the ministry of the Christian church. The bishop is to be chosen from proven paterfamilias in the community. Deacons should be like good adult sons of the paterfamilias, 'managing their children and households well'. Women who serve as deacons are to be like frugal housewives, 'serious, not slanderers, temperate and faithful in all things'.[29]

Although the author of 1 Timothy assumes a sphere of female ministry, he seeks to limit it; to confine it to elderly widows over 60 years of age, eliminating younger unmarried or widowed women. He is in conflict with what he sees as the too great independence of some group of these women who he describes as 'gadding about from house to house, gossips and busybodies, some having even become heretics, turning away 'to follow Satan'. He also decries what he calls 'profane myths and old wives' tales'.[30] It is likely that the target of these denunciations is precisely those groups of unmarried women ministers who lived together, serving to catechize and baptize women and visiting sick women in their homes.

What are the 'profane myths and old wives' tales'? Since what 1 Timothy condemns is women who speak, have authority over men, do not marry and are too independent in their ministering, it is likely

28. 1 Tim. 2.11-15.
29. 1 Tim. 3.2-12.
30. 1 Tim. 5.9-15.

that his opponents are Christians who hold something like the views found in the *Acts of Paul and Thecla*, where exactly such a woman is not only accepted but extolled with Paul's blessing.[31]

This second type of Christianity lost out in the battle for Pauline authority and was relegated to non-canonical status, while 1 Timothy not only made it into the canon, but became the defining lens for the Christian theology of gender for the future. But the belief that redemption in Christ overcomes gender hierarchy did not disappear from Christianity. It was continued in celibate women's communities from the early church down through the Middle Ages to today, that again and again have resisted the efforts of patriarchal church leaders to curtail their independence and confine them behind walls.

Also the remnants of the theology of equality in Christ remained in tantalizing remnants in the stories of the Gospels as well as the theological proclamations in the book of Acts and Paul's letter to the Galatians: 'Your sons and daughters shall prophesy,' 'In Christ no more male and female,' the song of Mary in Luke, 'The mighty shall be put down from their thrones and the poor lifted up.' These visions of iconoclastic reversal of social order, the exalting of those presently most despised in the dawning of God's Kingdom, a new community in Christ where all class, race and gender divisions are overcome, and all are one in Christ would be rediscovered again and again in movements of Christian renewal: Waldensians in the twelfth century: Baptists, Levelers and Quakers in seventeenth-century England, Christian women working for suffrage and the ordination or women in the nineteenth and twentieth centuries.

Like a buried but never quite extinguished explosive charge, this theology of new humanity in Christ, where all social hierarchy is overcome has continued to explode again and again in Christian history and its secularized offspring, pointing to a revolutionary vision of a redeemed society in which the original equality of all people in the image of God is restored.

31. See MacDonald 1983: 54-77.

Chapter Two

Conflicting Paradigms of Redemption and Gender in Patristic and Medieval Christianity

The legacy of Pauline Christianity was one of deep conflict over the relationship between redemption in Christ and gender hierarchy in society. One group of Christians who claimed Paul's authority took the baptismal theology of Gal. 3.28: 'In Christ no more male and female' to mean that the gender differences were annulled, the new age in which there shall be no more marrying or giving in marriage was spiritually present and women transformed in the Spirit could prophesy, teach and baptize. Other Pauline Christians read these texts as meaning only a spiritual equality that left gender roles unchanged in a still untransformed world. Wives are still to submit to their husbands; their secondary status in creation and primacy in sin means that they can enter redemption only through redoubled acceptance of the subjugation inherited from their sinful mother Eve. Against the Pentecostal proclamation, 'your sons and daughters shall prophesy' stood the apostle's command, 'Women, keep silence, even as the Law says.'[1]

This conflict was renewed in the second century. Daring new speculative theologians like Marcion saw the redeemed Christian community as related to a higher God of Love against an oppressive cosmocrator who rules over the world of war, punitive violence and death. Redeemed life in Christ rescues the believer from the rules and social divisions of this God of Law, including those between Jew and Greek, master and slave, men and women, the diseased and untouchables and those who regard themselves as 'the pure'. Marriage and procreation is part of the fallen world and so celibacy was encouraged. Marcionite

---

1.   Acts 2.17; 1 Cor. 14.34 and 1 Tim. 2.11-12.

churches practiced a discipleship of equals in which women taught, exorcised, healed and baptized.[2]

Valentinian gnosticism was another variant of radical egalitarian Christianity of the second century. Adamic fall and redemption in Christ was told through a story of cosmic devolution and reintegration into a higher divine world far above this lower world of ignorance and death. Valentinians saw this higher world as constituted by a series of divine male-female pairs ending in the cosmic Wisdom, who both causes the fallen world but also mediates the escape of those trapped within it. Reintegration into the higher world was seen as reclaiming one's androgynous unity from sexual dimorphism, rising above sex and procreation. Women not only could participate equally in the community of the redeemed, but were seen as representing a higher spiritual insight.[3] Mary Magdalene was held up as the beloved disciple closest to Christ through which the teachings of the risen Lord were conveyed to the male disciples, a view found in the Gospel of Mary.[4]

Other second-century Christians did not accept these cosmic speculations, but saw themselves as continuing a Christianity in which the Pentecostal outpouring of the gifts of the Spirit mandated prophetic teaching by women and men alike. A renewal of this view was represented in the second half of the century by the New Prophecy that arose in Phrygia, but soon had adherents in other areas of Asia, Gaul, Rome and North Africa. Two women, Prisca and Maximilla, along with Montanus, were honored as founding prophets. Preparing for the millennium soon to come, Montanist prophets practiced continence and fasting, discarded marriage relations and were itinerant preachers, while living in readiness for martyrdom.[5] Other second- and early third-century Christian leaders of what was constituting itself as the catholic church repudiated the challenges of the New Prophecy to its authority patterns, as well as speculative theologies of Marcionites and Valentinians. They insisted on a continuity of creation with redemption. The God who created the world is the same God who is redeeming it in Christ. Moreover this redemption, although begun in Christ and mediated in baptism, is not complete. This meant, for them, that the hierarchy of male

2.   For a new look at Marcion, see Hoffmann (1984).
3.   Clement, *Excerpta Ex Theodoto*; see also Layton (1980).
4.   'The Gospel of Mary', in Robinson (1977: 471-74).
5.   See Trevett 1996.

over female was mandated through some combination of the order of creation and Eve's greater guilt for the Fall. Women are not to throw off these ordinances of creation and punishment even though they are redeemed by Christ. Rather, women's submission is the means for her atonement.

The distance between second-century Catholics and these alternative Christianities was not so great as is often assumed. Some Catholic leaders, like the anti-gnostic bishop Irenaeus in southern Gaul, were sympathetic to the New Prophecy as a true expression of apostolic Christianity,[6] although he firmly opposed all gnostics. The acerbic Tertullian in North Africa would denounce Marcion and the gnostics, but himself pass over to Montanism.[7] Clement of Alexandria spoke of Christianity as a type of gnosis,[8] while Origen constructed a cosmology of devolution into bodily finitude and reascent through successive reincarnations into a disembodied heavenly world.[9] Sexual abstinence and readiness for martyrdom were extolled by both sides.

But the two sides parted company significantly on how redemption, baptism and the outpouring of the Spirit freed women for leadership roles. Tertullian, in his Montanist phase, would accept women's gifts of prophecy, but insist that women should exercise this gift only in private, to be conveyed to the public Christian assembly by duly recognized male authorities. Moreover, submission of women to male authority in family and church, as well as covered heads and figures signaling women's subjugation in creation and greater guilt for sin, are in no way altered for Christian women, but are to be the more strictly observed.[10]

The ascetic Origen, who comes close to gnosticism in his speculative cosmology and rejection of sex and the flesh, is also the most vehement in his rejection of women's public ministry. Female virgins may in no way claim public roles in the Christian assembly. In his commentary on 1 Cor. 14.34-36 Origen assailed the Montanist women prophets, reiterating Paul's command to 'keep silence in the churches'. Although Origen admits that prophetic gifts were sometimes given by God to women in biblical times, these gifts were exercised only in private, and

---

6.   Trevett 1996: 56.
7.   Trevett 1996: 66-76.
8.   See 'Clement of Alexandria', in von Campenhausen (1963: 25-36).
9.   Origen, *On First Principles*.
10. Tertullian, *On the Soul*; see also Trevett 1996: 68-69.

conveyed to the public assembly only when duly tested by accredited male authorities.[11]

This anthropology of women's subordination in creation redoubled by sin and still continuing in the church would be formulated in its classical form for western Christianity by Augustine in the late fourth and early fifth centuries. In Augustine's early writings on Genesis he followed a Philonic view of seeing humans as created first in incorporeal unity. The image of God refers not to the physical body, but to the 'interior man' or intellect through which humans rule the lower creation and contemplate eternal things. Creation male and female originally meant the union of spirit and soul, in which the male intellect ruled over the female psyche. This incorporeal human would have reproduced angelically and created 'spiritual offspring of intelligible and immortal joys'. Only after sin did the physical body, sexual differentiation and 'carnal fecundity' begin.[12]

But Augustine increasingly shifted from this Platonic view to one in which Adam and Eve were created with real physical and sexually differentiated bodies. Gender differentiation, sexual intercourse and physical offspring were part of God's original created design, and not simply features that appeared after sin and as a remedy for mortality. In these later writings Augustine taught that God originally created the idea of the human, the spiritual essence or image of God that both men and women possess equally, apart from their bodies, social and sexual functions and roles.

But, in the actual production of the human, the male was created first and then the female from his side, to indicate the relation of superiority and subordination by which the genders are to relate in their physical and social roles. For Augustine gender hierarchy is not simply the fruit of sin, but an integral part of God's original plan for creation, in respect to the gendered roles of men and women in sex, child bearing and social order, although this will have no place in heaven, when these roles have disappeared.[13]

Adam and Eve would originally not have died. They would have reproduced physically, but without physical orgasm or concupiscence. But with the Fall these privileges have disappeared. The Fall plunges

---

11. Origen, *Commentary on Romans* 10.17; and 'Fragments on I Cor' (Jenkins [ed.] 1907/1908). See Trevett 1996: 174-75.

12. Augustine, *Genesis against the Manichees*, 1.19, 30, in Teske (1991: 76-78).

13. See Børresen and Vogt 1995: 15-72.

humanity into sin and death, the loss of original immortality and the ability to obey God freely. Humans are now bound to sinful pride, unable to obey God as a free act of will. Their sexual relations are corrupted by sinful lust through which the legacy of sin is transmitted from parents to offspring.[14]

Although woman would have been subordinate in paradise, in the Fall this subordination has been worsened to servitude to be coercively enforced due to sinful resistance to the right obedience that women owe to their male head. This has not been changed for Christian women, even those who adopt the virginal life that anticipates the heavenly order. Although gender hierarchy will disappear in heaven, as long as earthly life persists, women must submit to male authority and have no public leadership roles. Indeed virginal women indicate their converted minds by willingly submitting to male authority and eschewing any will of their own.[15]

This Augustinian view would be passed on as orthodoxy into the Latin Middle Ages to be repeated in substantially the same form by Thomas Aquinas. Thomas, however, deepens the view of women's natural subordination by adopting the Aristotelian socio-biology that taught that women were biologically defective, lacking the fullness of human nature mentally, morally and physically, hence needing to be governed by men and incapable of exercising public leadership in either church or political life. Only the male possesses full and normative humanness. For Thomas this also has christological consequences. Christ had to be male in order to possess full human nature and to represent headship over the restored human race and only the male can represent Christ in the priesthood.[16]

In the late third and fourth centuries the tensions between married and celibate Christians, and the idea that virginity released women from patriarchal subordination was reinterpreted. A new ascetic Christianity emerged, linked to monks of the Egyptian and Judaean deserts. These monks became the new ideal of a radical Christian holiness. A new generation of Christian leaders arose, Athanasius and the Cappadocians, Basil, Gregory Nazianzus and Gregory Nyssa in the East and Ambrose

14. Augustine, *City of God* 14.22-26 and *On Grace and Free Will*, NPNF, 5: 44 (22).

15. *On Genesis against the Manichees* 2.19 and *On the Literal Interpretation of Genesis* 11.37.

16. See Børresen and Vogt 1995: 230-31, 235-38.

and Augustine in the West, who adopted the monastic life style and merged it with episcopal office. Women were enthusiastic supporters of the monks, and many flocked to adopt this life style themselves. Some, such as Macrina, the sister of Basil the Great and Gregory Nyssa, was herself the founder of monastic life in her family, drawing her brothers into what they called 'the philosophical life'. Gregory Nyssa would see Macrina as his own spiritual mentor in the pursuit of holiness.[17]

Among the Roman nobility there was a remarkable generation of female ascetic leaders and founders of monastic communities. These included Marcella, who founded a female ascetic community in Rome in the 350s. There was Melania the Elder, who adopted the ascetic life in Rome in 364 after the death of her husband left her a young widow. In 372 she left Rome for a tour of the monastic communities of Egypt and then settled in Jerusalem. Joined by Rufinus, the translator of Origen, she founded a monastic community for women and another for men, as well as a hospice for pilgrims on the Mount of Olives. Another member of Marcella's circle was Paula, a wealthy widow with five children, who, with her daughter Eustochium, left for the East about 385, joined by Jerome, where she founded three monastic communities for women and one for men, also with a pilgrim's hospice, in Bethlehem. These women passed down their monastic foundations to their female descendants. Paula's communities were led by her daughter Eustochium and then her granddaughter Paula Junior, while Melania's communities passed into the hands of her granddaughter Melania Junior.[18] Olympias, a wealthy heiress in Constantinople founded extensive monastic establishments there and was an ardent supporter of the embattled and then exiled bishop and theologian John Chrysostom.[19]

Although these women exercised considerable power through their independent wealth, and the prestige their rigorous life style commanded in Christian circles linked to the male ascetic leaders of their day, they nevertheless accepted the established dictum that women, even the holiest and most aristocratic, could exercise no public leadership. Celibacy was understood to dissolve their traditional roles in the family as reproducers and household managers, but their subordination to men was now transferred to church leaders. In the monastic idiom of

17. 'On the Life of Macrina' and 'On the Soul and the Resurrection', in Nyssa (1967: V, 161-272).

18. Ruether 1979a: 71-98; also Cloke 1995.

19. 'The Life of Olympias, Deacon', in Kraemer (1988); also Clark 1979.

the day, they were said to have discarded their weak femaleness and had become 'virile and manly'.

When these holy women departed from their homes to travel to visit monks and holy places in the East and then to found their own monastic establishments, funding those of their ascetic male partners as well, these roles were highly commended. But they were to exercise these leadership roles in strictest retirement, fasting and self-abasement, and deference to male authority in the church. They certainly were not to teach or preach in public, although males as well as females, even priests, might go to them for private teaching.[20]

One effect of this uniting of inward holiness and power and its strict privatization is that we have very little writing from any of these formidable women monastic leaders of the high patristic age. We know from their male colleagues, such as Jerome, that these women were eager scholars who studied Hebrew in order to read the Hebrew Scriptures in the original, read the writings of the church fathers, discussed points of exegesis in their circles and in letters and even intervened in theological disputes, such as that over the authority of Origen that set Rufinus, the partner of Melania, against Jerome, who was supported by Marcella.[21] Yet only a few letters, accidentally preserved in the letters of their male colleagues, are extant, giving us very little sense of their own thought.[22]

This situation of women's lack of teaching authority in the church continued officially in the Middle Ages and was renewed in the Reformation. But, for several reasons, its implications for lack of preservation and publication of women's religious writings began to change in practice in the tenth century with such works as the plays of Hrotswit of Gandersheim. Women's published writings grew in the eleventh century and became a mighty stream from the twelfth to the fifteen centuries.[23] Women were writing and publishing in a variety of genres, letters, plays and saint's lives, and also theological treatises, guides to spiritual life and above all accounts of their mystical experiences, which

20. Jerome, letter 127.7.

21. See Cloke 1995: 175-85.

22. A letter from Paula and Eustochium to Marcella and two letters from a Spanish female ascetic to a female colleague are preserved among the letters of Jerome. Eleven letters of Melania the Elder were transmitted in Armenian. See Børresen and Vogt 1995: 247, 270 nn. 9-11.

23. See Kadel 1995.

became the characteristic female genre of theological writing. These writings were circulated among both men and women and were highly respected as guides to God's will and the pursuit of the holy life. How did women gain a public voice in medieval Catholicism? and how did their writings began to reshape the terms of understanding the relation of gender and redemption theologically?

The primary reason that medieval women were able to write and have these writings circulated and preserved was the creation of female-ruled religious communities. Female religious communities gave women the rudiments of literacy. There they had libraries, scriptoria that often included illumination, where their thoughts could be written down and preserved, copied and circulated to other readers. Through liturgical prayer and through study women could gain an extensive knowledge of scripture and some theology and express themselves in writings on the spiritual life that were read and preserved by their communities.

Medieval women gained authority for a public voice as writers, teachers and sometimes preachers in the ruling church primarily by evoking a legacy inherited from the New Testament, namely, the idea that, although women could not be priests, they could be prophets. God might speak directly to a woman, conveying an urgent message to the church and society of her time. Women might experience God in reve-latory disclosures that could not only direct her but others on the path of holiness. In these roles as direct vehicles of God's presence and voice, women both denounced evils and pointed the way to restored life with God.

But the medieval women's revelatory experiences were not self-vali-dating. They must be validated by male church authority, the higher the rank the better. This might start with a male confessor but he in turn might be able to draw in support from an abbot of a related male order, a bishop and even the Pope. Visionary women who failed to gain such male church support could hardly gain a voice. When churchmen were divided on a woman's prophetic authenticity, who won determined whether a woman's writings were circulated and preserved or suppressed and even burned along with herself. When a woman claimed revelations, the critical question was: 'From whence come these revela-tion, God or the Devil?' Was she a prophet or a heretic or even a witch, and which men had the power to make the decision?

I will discuss here three significant medieval visionary women of the many that wrote their religious experiences from the twelfth to the sixteenth centuries, each of whom lived and worked in a different kind of religious setting. The first is Hildegard of Bingen, a powerful German abbess whose life spanned the twelfth century from 1098 to 1179. The second is Mechtild of Magdeburg in the thirteenth century, who lived most of her life as a beguine, a new form of urban religious life where women took only simple vows and were not cloistered, working for a living and providing services to their towns, such as nursing and teaching. This kind of religious life fell under deep suspicion from male church authorities as allowing women too great independence, and Mechtild fled at the end of her life to live with the powerful and learned nuns of Helfta, who honored and supported her in her writing. The third figure is Julian of Norwich, born in that thriving English city in 1342 and living into the fifteenth century. Although Julian may have been educated in a convent, most of her religious life was spent as an anchoress attached to the parish church, where she not only organized her own religious life but served as a counselor to others who came to her for advice, among them the lay woman mystical writer Margery of Kempe.

In claiming their authority to speak and write publicly, each of these three women follow a typical pattern. They accept and even emphasize their lack of authority as women, while proclaiming that this female weakness has been overcome by God, who has chosen to speak to them and commanded them to write what God said. They use Pauline texts that declare that God chooses the weak things of the world to confound the mighty to explicate this reversal of women's lack of authority. This was a powerful way of validating a gospel vision of a God who does not support but reverses the power hierarchies of this world, including those of the church.

Hildegard of Bingen habitually affirms her prophetic authority by referring to herself as a 'poor little female figure' (paupercula feminea forma), physically weak, unlearned and without status as a daughter of fallen Eve, but speaking with a thunderous voice to the greatest men of her day as the vehicle of divine revelation and judgment.[24] Hildegard, who was well connected through powerful noble German families, successfully won over the highest male authorities to validate the authenticity of her prophetic claims. She first confided her visions to her female mentor Jutta, and then the monk Volmar, who recommended

---

24. The term appears as formulaic in Hildegard's letters to her correspondents and other writings. For a discussion, see Newman (1987: 1-41).

her to Kuno, the abbot of the adjoining male monastery. She also sent her writing to the greatest monastic authority of her day, Bernard of Clairvaux. Kuno told the Archbishop of Mainz of Hildegard's writings, who informed the Pope Eugenius III, then meeting in synod in Germany. Bernard commended Hildegard to the Pope, who happened to be a Cistercian. The Pope read her writings and affirmed the authenticity of her prophetic gift. Thus Hildegard, by a combination of good connections and diplomacy, was credentialed by the highest church authorities.[25] This allowed her to claim great freedom to speak, denouncing the evils of her day and laying forth her visions of theological cosmology from creation to eschatology, even conducting several preaching tours through Germany.

Mechtild, while far less well connected than Hildegard, followed a similar pattern of protesting her female unworthiness and lack of learning, but affirming that God's command that she write his disclosures takes precedence over her weakness. She too won male support through her Dominican confessor, Heinrich of Halle, as well as aristocratic female support from the nuns of Helfta. For Mechtild, God's choice of such a lowly vessel for these visions duplicates the kenosis of God in the incarnation. God typically imparts special graces to the lowest and least, as a mighty flood flows by nature into the valley. She also echoes Paul's dictums that God chooses the lowly to confound the wise.[26]

Julian of Norwich likewise describes herself as 'a woman, ignorant, feeble and frail', but nevertheless commanded by God to teach the people through her visions, not to exalt herself, but to be an instrument of benefit for the Christian people. As she puts it, 'Because I am a woman should I therefore believe that I ought not to tell you about the goodness of God since I saw at the same time that it is his will that it be known?'[27] For her the answer to this hypothetical question was clearly 'No'.

Women were also given a solid sense of their own religious authority through their reading of Christian theology. Although they acknowledged their weakness as women, they generally do so in terms of physical frailty and lack of learning compared to male theologians of their day. But for these women their inner nature as image of God is their essential nature, while their femaleness *qua* weakness and unworthiness is

---

25. See Hildegard's letters 1 and reply and 2 (Baird and Ehrman 1994: 28-33).
26. von Magdeburg 1991: 56-57.
27. Colledge and Walsh 1978: Chapter 6, short text.

accidental and unimportant. Vis-à-vis God these women speak of themselves, not as of lesser worth as women, but simply as human, as soul or spiritual self with no less capacity for spiritual life and holiness than another human who might happen to inhabit a male body.

So Hildegard, when she reports God's address to her or when she addresses others as God's prophet, speaks of herself simply as 'homo', man, the essential human being made in the image of God,[28] not as 'a poor weak female form'. Mechtild and Julian likewise understand their essential selves as the inner spiritual self, the soul, made in the image of God, equally heir to divine redemption, of no lesser worth in the heavenly economy of creation and redemption. As those who are pursuing holiness through ascetic discipline and contemplative prayer, they are also those who are in the way of full restoration of their created image of God to its original and fulfilled goodness. Thus these women acknowledge an accidental weakness as women, one that has been overcome by divine power, but no essential inferiority.

These women follow the path laid out by earlier Christian asceticism by which women annul their weak femaleness through celibacy and asceticism that restores them to their essential non-gendered humanness as *imago Dei*. But they add a second way of reconciling femaleness and godliness. They begin to develop positive female symbolism that expresses in female imagery the spiritual life of the soul and the nature and work of God.

These developments in medieval women mystics were not without some precedents in biblical and early Christian thought. Mystical Judaism and some lines of early Christianity developed the Wisdom theme of the female personification of God manifest in the creation and sustaining of nature and in revelation. The soul in relation to God and the church married to Christ had long been symbolized as female, the bridal soul, the bride of Christ and Mother Church.[29] Christ imaged himself as like a mother hen who wishes to gather her chicks under her wings, and the early church spoke of baptism and eucharist in language of the

---

28. For example, in the *Scivias*, God commands Hildegard thus: 'Tu ergo, o homo . . . scribe quae vides et audis' (Furhkotter 1978: XLIII, 5, ll. 75-78).

29. For the wisdom theme, see Wisdom of Solomon. The union of the feminine soul and the church with Christ was developed particularly from the patristic and medieval readings of the Song of Songs: see Origen, *Commentary on the Song of Songs*. For the identification of Wisdom with Mary, see Ruether (1979b: 20-24).

womb, birth and feeding from the mother's breast.[30]

Hildegard, Mechtild and Julian draw on and further develop these resources of positive female imagery for God, creation and the self. Hildegard developed a theological cosmology from creation to the final transformation of the world that is characterized by positive female complementarity at each stage. In creation, God and God's word are imaged as masculine, and flesh, matter and earth (Terra) as female, not as evil principles, but as that good bodily substance that God creates and fills with God's spirit, the power of vivifying life Hildegard speaks of as 'greenness' ('viriditas'). The beauty and goodness of God's creation consists in the harmonious union of these two principles, God's life-giving spirit and virgin Terra.[31]

The creating and redeeming union of God and creation is mediated for Hildgard by two powerful cosmic forces, Sapientia (Wisdom) and Caritas (Love). Through Sapientia and Caritas, seen as personified female cosmic powers, God both creates the cosmos and the human and continually renews their relation to God through incarnation and the redemptive work of the Church. The axis of this union of God with flesh mediated by Wisdom and Love is the incarnation of the Word in the flesh of the Virgin Mary, who represents unfallen virginal flesh totally united with the divine Spirit.[32] The culminating female figure of Hildegard's symbolic theology is Ecclesia, Bride of Christ and Mother of Christians, who receives the vivifying power of Christ's redemptive sacrifice on the cross as her bridal 'dowry'. Ecclesia is pictured in Hildegard's vision as a towering woman holding reborn Christians in her protecting arms and womb, while her head is assailed by sinful and

---

30. Eucharistic imagery of feeding Christians milk has its New Testament locus particularly in 1 Cor. 3.2, but it was also developed from early Christian baptismal liturgies where the baptized first received a cup of milk and honey: see *The Apostolic Tradition*, in Connelly (1916: 84). The theme of Christ feeding Christians at the breast is often combined with images of feeding from his side with blood. The mingling of blood/milk imagery was supported by the view in ancient medicine that the mother's milk is transformed blood. See Franklin (1978: 137-45).

31. See Hildegard, *Book of Divine Works I*, vision 4, on the micro-macrocosmic relations of the human body-soul relations and the cosmos (Santa Fe, NM: Bear, 1987).

32. Hildegard, *Book of Divine Works II*, vision 1, on Wisdom in Creation; *III*, vision 8, on Love; and vision 9, on creation as Wisdom's garment. Vision 1 also parallels the Virgin Earth and the body of the Virgin Mary.

corrupt male church leaders.[33] Female Christian virgins are the fullest expression of the true children of Mother Church, in whom the union of God and creation is restored and paradise anticipated, particularly in their sweet voices raised in choral song.[34]

Mechtild similarly focuses her theology on positive female imagery, particularly the soul, seen as bride and lover of Christ whom God woos and seeks union with, even abasing himself in suffering in order to win her to himself. Mechtild draws on the rich imagery of courtly love, and the biblical Song of Songs to describe this many faceted love relation of God and the soul.[35]

Finally Julian draws together these different aspects of the feminine symbol: as soul in relation to God, as body both suffering and renewed, expressing humanness in its vulnerability and the flesh that Christ takes to himself, and finally the Wisdom imagery of God, to incorporate the feminine into the Trinitarian nature of God. The second person of the Trinity especially expresses the mother nature of God, both in God's loving graciousness in creating and restoring our 'substantial' or spiritual nature and also in our 'sensuality' or flesh, which Christ assumes and renews in its union with God. Thus Julian says of God:

> God in our making is our kindly father and God all-wisdom is our kindly mother, with the love and goodness of the Holy Spirit...for I saw that the second person who is our Mother substantially is now our Mother sensually... The second person of the Trinity is our Mother in our substantial making, in whom we are grounded and rooted, and he is our Mother of mercy in taking our sensuality... Thus Jesus Christ who does good against evil is our very Mother. We have our being of him, where every ground of Motherhood begins, with all the sweet keeping of love that endlessly follows. As truly as God is our Father, so truly is God our Mother.[36]

Thus despite the authoritative way in which Christian women were defined as subjected in creation, reduced to servitude through sin and

33. Hildegard, *Scivias*, II, visions 4, 5 and 6; see English edition edited by Hart and Bishop (1990: 187-238).

34. Hildegard's defense of her practices of robing her nuns in white garments with gold crowns in liturgy shows the way she sees such liturgy as anticipation of paradise restored and heavenly bliss; see her letter 52R, Baird and Ehrman (1994: 128-30).

35. For the imagery of courtly love in Mechthild, see Newman (1995: 137-67).

36. Julian of Norwich, chs. 58-59, long text (Colledge and Walsh 1978: 159-61).

commanded to be silent as members of the body of Christ, these women, convinced that they are truly equal in creation and redemption, overcame these restrictions and gained a voice as prophet, teacher and mentor in salvation. The possibility of claiming this voice was supported by the partial autonomy of female-identified communities. They were empowered by the elements in Christian theology that conceded that women were ultimately equally human before God, as *imago Dei* restored in Christ, and also that they might be gifted by direct divine revelations.

Visionary Christian not only availed themselves of these openings for religious authority, but also began to overcome the gender symbolism that made God and the higher spiritual powers of the self male, while linking femaleness only with finitude, sex and sin. In their visions gender became fluid and transformative, the male descending into the female and the female arising into the male, until not only the human but God was recognized as both male and female.[37]

37. For the importance of Julian's incorporation of female metaphors into the Trinitarian nature of God, see Børresen and Vogt (1995).

Chapter Three

Conflicting Paradigms of Redemption and Gender in the Reformation Era

The Reformation era of the sixteenth–seventeenth centuries was an ambiguous one for women. On the one hand, the Reformers challenged Roman Catholic male clericalism in ways that seemed egalitarian, such as the principle of the priesthood of all believers. Their sweeping away of the system of celibacy and monastic life overcame the hierarchy of the celibate over the married, elevating the status of marriage. They redefined the idea of vocation to mean a person's work in society, not a calling out of society. They encouraged lay literacy and Bible reading.

But many of these changes, while opening up opportunities for men, were restrictive for women. A male could now combine marriage and ministry, but the female was still told that she could not speak in church. The female communities that gave women spheres of learning, leadership and religious life were swept away, at times against the determined resistance of nuns, who objected when their way of life was denigrated rather than honored.[1] While a man's work in the world was now seen as his calling from God, women were defined as having only one calling, to be wife and mother. New schools opened for boys, but little for girls, while the women's communities that had educated females were destroyed. Veneration of Mary and women saints were overthrown, giving Protestantism a much more severely masculine symbol system and religious leadership.[2]

At the same time the overall legal, social and economic systems in Catholic and Protestant regions were limiting women's sphere much

1. For an example of a learned abbess of Nuremberg who opposed the efforts of the Reformers in that city to close her community, see Barker (1995).
2. See Weisner 1988.

more strictly to the home (or to a cloistered convent, in the Catholic case) than had been the case in the medieval world, where women played larger work and political roles according to class. Guilds were restricting almost all skilled work, such as brewing, baking, silver-work and even textiles, to men, confining women to low-paying occasional work.[3]

Legal and political changes made women more strictly dependent on a male guardian, even if unmarried or a widow, eliminating political roles that women had played as property-holders.[4] Yet the sixteenth century, owing to lack or minority of male heirs in several royal houses, had a significant number of powerful queens.[5] The visible power of a few women, together with an overall restriction of most women, made this a time of vehement argument over the nature and role of women.

The fifteenth through the seventeenth centuries saw a flourishing literature pro and contra women, arguing whether women were primarily evil and a misfortune to men or rather possessed equal and even superior virtues. A typical list of good and bad women from biblical and classical history were marshaled to make the argument on one side or the other. The misogynist literature was popular with men and had a definite effect, not only in justifying women's subjugation in the family and exclusion from public roles, but also wife beating.[6]

Witch-hunting was also renewed in the Reformation era, running rampant in the contested Catholic and Protestant areas of Germany, but also found in other areas. In Protestantism Calvinism seemed to lend itself particularly to witch-hunting. One has from Puritan divines, such as William Perkins, both the *Christian Oeconomie* (1590) on the proper roles of women and men in marriage and *On the Damned Art of Witchcraft* (1596), arguing that the witch should be killed, with no mercy on account of her weak female nature.[7]

Gender and Redemption in Luther and Calvin

The Protestant reformers generally repeated the traditional Augustinian view of women, but contesting realities gave this an added edge. John

---

3. See Weisner 1986; also Herlihy 1990.
4. See Weisner 1993: 30-34.
5. Hopkins 1991.
6. See Henderson and McManus 1985; see also Engel 1992.
7. See Perkins 1970.

Knox's *First Blast of the Trumpet against the Monstrous Regiment of Women* (1558) polemicized against female political rule as unnatural, contrary to Scripture and divine ordinances of creation, against Mary Queen of Scots and Mary Tudor, having then to live down the enmity of Elizabeth I.[8]

Luther and Calvin's views of women's place in the orders of Creation, the condition of sin and the grace of redemption follow the traditional lines. Luther pioneered the Reformation attack on celibacy and the insistence that all should marry. The creation of humanity, male and female, at the beginning signals God's intention that marriage and procreation are normative for all women and almost all men. Luther concedes that a few men might be 'naturally celibate', but this is very rare. God created women primarily to be wives and mothers. As Luther puts it in his 1519 sermon on marriage, 'A woman is created to be a companionable helpmeet to the man in everything, particularly to bear children.'[9]

In paradise Adam and Eve would have been physically, morally and mentally perfect. They would have embraced each other lovingly without shame or lust. Eve would have had no pain in childbearing and would have been much more fertile, having many more children than women today. These children would have been born more mature, standing up and walking immediately. But even in paradise Eve's primary role was to be wife and mother.

Household government of man over woman was established already in paradise, although woman would have shared more equally in the administration of the household than now. But civil government would have been unnecessary because there would have been no war or crime. Eve was similar to Adam in her interior nature as image of God. Nevertheless she would have been lesser as woman. As Luther puts it, 'Even as the sun is more excellent than the moon, so the woman, although she was a most beautiful work of God, nevertheless was not the equal of the male in glory and prestige.'[10]

In paradise there would have been no sin, disease or death, and even annoyances like flies would have been absent. Adam and Eve would have lived a much longer life and then fallen asleep to be taken to

8. Knox 1985. See also Smith 1920: 361.
9. Martin Luther, 'Sermon on the Estate of Marriage', in Atkinson (1966: XLIV, 8).
10. Martin Luther, 'Lectures on Genesis', in Atkinson (1966: I, 68-69).

heaven along with their many children. But this was not to be. Satan approached the woman as the weaker and more light-minded and she succumbed to temptation, even 'offering herself to Satan as his pupil'.[11]

With the Fall man and woman, together with the whole creation, lost their original perfection. Adam is punished by hard labor in a thorny earth, while Eve must now suffer in childbirth and be under the dominion of her husband. While formerly she would have been his willing but subordinate companion, now she is under servitude and is much more restricted to the home, while the fields of civil government and war are opened up to the male. As Luther puts it:

> He rules the home and the state, wages war, defends his possessions, tills the soil and plants. The wife, on the other hand, is like a nail driven into the wall. She sits at home . . . In this way Eve is punished.[12]

Luther follows Augustine in teaching that a cardinal effect of the Fall is the corruption of human sexuality into lust. Luther speaks of sex in its present form as like a disease, comparing it to an epileptic fit, but this is no reason to avoid it, but rather is the reason why it is now doubly necessary for all, since without marriage all (men?) would be driven by lust to sin.[13] Thus woman is God's gift to man, not only for companionship and offspring, but as antidote to sin, confining one's lust to one's legal wife.

Calvin's anthropology comes out in much the same place as Luther's, although he thinks of woman's secondary status in creation and subjugation in sin in more juridical terms. In spiritual nature before God Eve shared equally in the image of God and therefore has the same possibility of being elected to salvation. There is no gender discrimination in the economy of redemption to immortal life ordained by God from the beginning. But, in that distinct aspect of the image of God than has to do with dominion over lesser things, the rule is given to the male and woman is included under those things which are to be ruled.[14]

Even in paradise the woman is given to the man as helpmeet, and he is to be her head and leader. But this unequal partnership would have been harmonious since each would have accepted their place in the

11. Atkinson 1966: I, 81–82, 151, 162.

12. Atkinson 1966: I, 202-203.

13. Atkinson 1966: I, 119, 134.

14. John Calvin, *Commentaries on the Book of Genesis*, in King (1847: I, 96, 129-30). See also Thompson 1988.

divinely appointed order. The Fall, which Calvin attributes particularly to woman's insubordination, has disrupted this harmony. Hence woman must now be ruled coercively. Sex has been corrupted by lust, so marriage is doubly necessary, both for procreation and offspring and to prevent immorality. Now, as Calvin puts it, 'We are doubly subject to woman's society.'[15]

For both Luther and Calvin, redemption in Christ does not alter this subordination worsened to servitude by the Fall. Rather the Christian woman voluntarily submits to it, for the sake of an ultimate salvation that awaits her in heaven when these ordinances of creation and punishment will be transcended. Luther and Calvin are aware of the traditions of female prophecy in Scripture and of ruling queens in their own day.

Luther insists that women prophets in biblical times would have done so only in private, while Calvin sees God as being in command of his own ordinances and therefore being able to suspend them in times of crisis in the biblical era. Neither think God is likely to send any prophetesses in their own times. Luther has no place for female sovereigns, while Calvin suggests that this might be allowed rarely, but is itself a testimony to rampant sin among men, which God punishes through the humiliation of obeying a woman.[16]

Humanists and Left-Wing Christians on Gender and Redemption

Significant alternatives to these dominant views about women's place in creation, sin and redemption are found primarily among two groups in the sixteenth and seventeenth centuries: some humanists who take the pro-woman side of the debate about women, and left-wing Christians in England.

One of the most interesting contributions to the pro-woman side of the debate was written by a German humanist, Cornelius Agrippa von Nettlesheim, in 1509, 'On the Nobility and Superiority of the Female Sex'. In this treatise Agrippa turned the traditional arguments from Genesis upside-down. He starts by accepting the traditional claim that women and men were equal in the image of God in the original cre-

15. John Calvin, *Institutes of the Christian Religion*, in McNeil (1960: 130).

16. Martin Luther, 'Commentary on I Timothy', in Atkinson (1966: XXVIII, 276-77). Also John Calvin, 'Commentary on I Timothy', in Pringle (1856: 67-68).

ation, but then claims that in those things that have to do with her specific femaleness woman is superior to man.[17]

Agrippa points out that Eve's name means life while Adam means dirt, showing that the male is closer than the female to inert matter. He also suggests that Eve's name echoes the name of God and reflects the female aspect of God as Wisdom. Adam was created outside paradise, while Eve was created in paradise, and she was created from better stuff, living flesh and bone, rather than clay. Her creation after Adam means she is the crown of creation, the culminating work of God.

It was Adam, not Eve, who received the order not to eat of the fruit of the tree of life, and so he was more guilty of disobeying this command. Satan approached Eve first, not because she was weaker, but because he was jealous of her greater beauty and perfection. Moreover Christ came as a male because the male was more in need of redemption than the female. Woman's moral superiority is indicated by the enmity that God puts between her and the serpent, and this is fulfilled in the birth of Christ from Mary, whose perfection comes from having been the son of a woman without help from the male.

Agrippa goes on to detail all the noble women prophets and leaders of the Old Testament and the Gospels, culminating in the women disciples, led by Mary Magdalene, who are faithful to Christ at the cross when the male disciples run away and betray him. The gospel message was given first to women, who have been more faithful to it and carried it forward through the centuries. The right to preach was given to women at Pentecost, and Christian women taught in church. Christ came to overcome the hierarchy of male over female, and to restore women's equality with men.

For Agrippa the domination of men over women is due neither to female inferiority or divine will, but rather to male tyranny, which has usurped authority over women, even using religion for this purpose, justifying their tyranny by means of a misuse of sacred scripture. As Agrippa puts it:

> Thanks to the excessive tyranny of men, prevailing against divine right and the laws of nature, the freedom given to women is now banished by unjust laws, abolished by custom and usage and extinguished by upbringing. For as soon as a woman is born, she is kept at home in idleness from her earliest years, and as if incapable of higher employment, she is allowed to conceive nothing beyond her needle and thread... Public

17. Heinrich Cornelius Agrippa von Nettlesheim (Bene 1990).

offices too are denied her by law. No matter how intelligent, she is not allowed to plead in court… So great is the wickedness of recent legislators that they have made void the command of God for the sake of their traditions, as they pronounce women, who in other eras were more noble by virtue of their natural excellence and dignity, to be of baser condition than all men. By these laws therefore women are forced to yield to men like a conquered people to their conquerors in war, not compelled by any natural or divine necessity or reason, but rather by custom, education, fortune and tyrannical device.[18]

Agrippa believes that male domination is recent, while women in earlier pagan and even medieval times, such as great abbesses and queens, had greater dignity and power. He pleads' for a dissolution of these unjust laws and the restoration to women of their rightful place in political and cultural leadership 'with which God and nature have invested them'. Agrippa's treatise was popular in the sixteenth and seventeenth centuries, although almost unknown today. It was translated into Italian, French, German and English and often reprinted in these two centuries.

Writers, including many women who took the pro-woman side of the *querelle des femmes* knew his treatise and reproduced many of his arguments. For example, in 1615 in England one Joseph Swetnam wrote a popular tract, *The Arraignment of Lewd, Froward and unconstant women*, arguing for women's inferiority and evilness. This drew four responses from women writers, all published in 1617: from Ester Sowernam, Constantia Munda and Joan Sharpe (all probably pseudonymns) and Rachel Specht, the young daughter of an Evangelical minister.[19]

All three use Agrippa's arguments about Eve's greater dignity in creation and downplay her fault for sin. They suggest that Adam caused the Fall by railing against Eve and accusing her before God. Adam is the type of all misogynist men who disrupt the harmonious relations of the sexes and cause the loss of paradise by accusing women in order to exculpate themselves. These women also detail the great prophetesses of the Hebrew and Christian Scriptures and the faithfulness of women at the cross when the male disciples had deserted their Lord.

Ester Sowernam sums up her argument thus:

> Thus out of…the Old and New Testaments, I have observed in proofe of the worthiness of our sexe: First, that woman was the last worke of creation, I dare not say the best; she was created out of the chosen and

18. See Newman 1995: 230-39.
19. Henderson and McManus 1985: 189-216; also Spreght 1617.

> best refined substance; she was created in a more worthy country...her husband was enjoyed to a most inseperable and affectionate care over her; there is inseparable hatred and enmity put between the woman and the Serpent; Her first name, Eva, doth presage the nature and disposition of all women, not only in respect to their bearing, but further for the life and delight of the heart and soul of all mankinde. I have further showed the gratious, blessed and rarest benefits bestowed upon woman; all plainly out of Scripture. All of which doth demonstrate the blasphemous impudencie of the author of the Arraignment who would or durst write so basely and shamefully, in so general a manner, against our so worthy and honored a sexe.[20]

Unlike Agrippa, however, these women writers do not carry the argument into a denunciation of male tyranny in political affairs or argue for women's admission to public life. Rather they extol women's goodness and innocence primarily to argue that men should honor and value women as their wives and care for them with the greatest affection, rather than cruelly assailing them. They hold up an gentler view of patriarchal marriage in which the husband cares for and respects his wife, while the wife accepts this care from a husband who is both protector and friend.

In addition to these pro-women writers in the debate over women, seventeenth-century England also saw a significant number of upper-class women who cultivated study and writing in their homes in circles of learned women, drawing on the opportunities among the wealthy for tutors and family libraries. All these women were shut out of the possibility of university education. Although some sent their work to the learned men of their day, they were mostly scorned as eccentrics or blue stockings.[21] These women do not argue directly for opening universities to women or changing laws that cut women out of economic and political life. But they do begin to plead for women's expanded education in women's colleges.

One important figure in this circle of learned Anglican women was Mary Astell. She denounced marriage as oppressive, suggesting that the woman who wishes to study remain unmarried. Lacking a religious order as an institution for such unmarried women, Mary Astell proposed the creation of women's colleges that would also be places of religious life where learned celibate women could live and teach.[22]

20. Henderson and McManus 1985: 227.
21. See Smith 1982; also Ferguson 1985.
22. See Perry 1986.

Mary Astell developed a theology of women's spiritual and intellectual equality to sustain her argument for women's education, drawing on her study and correspondence with the Cambridge Platonists, particularly John Norris, who published their correspondence under the title of *Letters Concerning the Love of God* (1695). Astell never argued for women's political rights, and accepted gender and class hierarchy in society as a given. But she claims that women are spiritual equals to men, and this spiritual equality demands cultivation of the mind. Only through disciplined religious and intellectual life can the intellectual soul ascend into ever more perfect communion with God. By denying women the opportunity to study, men are denying women the right to cultivate their souls for the fullness of life both here and hereafter, to which women are equally called by God.[23]

In addition to the pro-woman humanist tradition, seventeenth-century England saw an expansion of women preachers and writers among radical Christian groups. The Civil War era saw a great outpouring of apocalyptic preachers claiming prophetic inspiration, including many women. At least 38 women prophets are known by name to have been preaching between the 1640s and early 1650s, most of them Baptists.[24] These women and men modeled their language after the books of Daniel and Revelations and saw themselves as crying out to the nation to repent before the time of Christ's imminent return as avenging judge.

One such prophetess and popular pamphleteer was Mary Cary, who published a series of visionary writings that applied the language of biblical apocalyptic to contemporary English politics. In her 1647 *A Word in Season to the Kingdom of England* Cary declared that God had delivered England from the grip of Satan through the defeat of the Royalists and execution of King Charles. God now expected the new leaders to bear good fruit. If they would avoid divine displeasure, Parliament and the Magistrates should stop oppressing the poor and mistreating God's prophets, such as herself, that were preaching the gospel. All should submit to the yoke of Christ as their true King.[25]

Cary and other Civil War prophetesses make the case for women's right to preach by declaring that the Holy Spirit is no respecter of persons. God gives the spirit of prophecy to women equally with men, to rebuke erring kings and prelates. God does not tie up the Spirit in

23. Astell 1970: 64–67.
24. Mack 1992: 413–14.
25. Cary 1647. See also Ruether 1990.

law nor confine it to priests, Levites or the learned. Rather God empowers the lowly and puts down the mighty. As Cary puts it, 'I am but a weak instrument, but I am all by the power of the Lord.'[26] Cary puts special emphasis on Acts 2.17-18. These are those last days in which God is pouring forth the Spirit and his sons and daughters shall prophesy. There is a short time for repentance before God comes in judgment, destroying the servants of Satan and delivering the saints now suffering to reign over a redeemed earth.

This type of prophecy faded with the end of the Civil War, but its spirit was inherited by the Quakers or Society of Friends, begun by George Fox in 1647. The Quakers spread rapidly in the 1660s, uniting radical witness in society with a disciplined familial community. Most Quakers came from the yeoman and small artisan classes. But some were former servants and a few from the landed gentry, such as Margaret Fell, who was converted by Fox and later married him, converting her home, Swarthmore Hall, into the organizational and communications base for the new Quaker movement.

Quaker life encouraged literacy among women as well as men. Quaker women's meetings kept careful records, noting their decisions and disbursements, and circulating exhortations to other women's meetings. Quakers networked with each other through letters, journals and travel diaries, intended for community reading. Women as well as men wrote tracts defending their theology, witnessing against persecution and calling kings, prelates and magistrates to account. These writings were put into printed form by Quaker presses and carefully preserved. Of the 650 Quaker authors whose writings are preserved from the first 50 years, 82 are women, some authoring numerous and lengthy tracts.[27]

Margaret Fell herself wrote 25 tracts, letters and journals, including her best-known work defending women's right to ministry, *Women's Preaching Justified according to the Scriptures* (1666). Quaker women in the seventeenth century were empowered by their church to go on extensive preaching and missionary journeys and to participate in the pastoral and administrative work of the local community. Through the women's meetings women held parallel leadership to men, particularly in the areas of moral discipline, supervision of marriage, the care for the poor, widows with children, the sick, infirm and elderly and those in prison.

26. Cary 1651: Preface; see Ruether 1990: 7-8.
27. See Mack 1992: 171.

They also administered the funds for these activities.[28]

Quaker women as much as men were often beaten and imprisoned for these preaching activities, and many of their tracts are written from prison, both as witnesses against the persecuting authorities and to inform their families and communities of their welfare. Indeed Quaker women sometimes suffered the brunt of a sadistic treatment from authorities who found their calm faith and unbending determination even more aggravating in a woman.

These active roles in local and itinerant ministry were supported by a Quaker theology of spiritual equality of women and men in God's creation, restored in Christ. The Quakers accepted the traditional Christian view that women were created equally in the image of God, but they rejected the qualifying claim that God established in paradise a rule of man over woman in respect to their particular sexual, reproductive and social roles. The domination of man over woman found in society they regarded, not as an expression of either original nature or punishment for women's greater responsibility for sin, but rather as an expression of unjust tyranny. Such domination reflects the fallen condition of humanity, which has lost its original spiritual power.

For the redeemed restored to spiritual power this domination has been overcome. As one Quaker writer puts it, Adam and Eve were originally created

> of one mind and soul and spirit, as well as one flesh, not usurping authority over each other...and the women was not commanded to be in subjugation to her husband until she was gone from the power...the power and image and spirit of God is the same authority in the female as in the male.[29]

Margaret Fell, in her *Women's Speaking Justified according to the Scriptures* develops this theology of gender equality with particular emphasis on women's right to preach.[30]

Not only did God originally 'put no such difference between male and female as men would make', but with the Fall God showed special mercy to Eve as the more innocent of the pair and the more truthful in confessing her fault to God, while Adam tried to blame both Eve and

---

28. For a seventeenth-century account of the work of Quaker women's meetings, see 'A Seventeenth Century Quaker Women's Declaration', in Speizman and Kronich (1975).

29. Mack 1992: 242.

30. Fell 1989.

God for his disobedience. Moreover God's curse upon the serpent put special enmity between 'the seed of the woman and the seed of the Serpent'. Following the tradition that the 'seed of the woman' is Christ, Quakers divided humanity between the 'two seeds', those who are in the light, who belong to the 'seed of the woman', and those who remain alienated from God, who belong to the seed of Satan.

It is those who belong to the seed of Satan who oppose women's preaching and spiritual authority, while God not only allows but commands the spiritually renewed woman to speak, for if she does not speak, Satan's voice will prevail. As Fell puts it:

> Let this word of the Lord which was from the beginning stop the mouths of all that oppose women's speaking in the power of the Lord. For he hath put enmity between the woman and the Serpent, and if the seed of the woman speak not, the seed of the Serpent speaks, for God hath put enmity between the two seeds. And it is manifest that those that speak against the woman and her seed speaking speak out of the enmity of the old serpent's seed.[31]

Even in the age of the Law God empowered women to speak as prophets, but with the coming of Christ the power of Satan has been dealt the decisive blow, and God's spirit has been poured out on all flesh, empowering both women and men to prophesy. Also Christ appeared first to women, making them apostles of the resurrection to the male apostles, who lacked the same steadfast faith. So redemption itself hinges on the willingness of men and women to accept 'the message of the Lord God that he sends by a woman', and hence the acceptance of women's preaching. In Fell's words:

> What had become of the redemption of the whole body of mankind if they had not believed the message that the Lord Jesus sent by these women, of and concerning his resurrection... Thus the Lord Jesus hath manifested himself and his power without respect of persons. And so let all mouths be stopped that would limit him, whose power and Spirit is infinite, that is pouring it upon *all* flesh.[32]

When confronted with the Pauline texts against women's preaching, Fell and other Quakers had a ready explanation. These texts refer to women who had not yet been redeemed, who had not yet received the power of the Spirit. Such women, and men too, who have not yet re-

31. Fell 1989.
32. Fell 1989: 8, 12.

ceived the Light, including bishops and other 'hireling priests', should indeed keep silence and listen to those who have received the Light. But for those who have received the Spirit, women as much as men, they can and must speak so Word of the Lord be known. Thus Quaker theology made a decisive shift in the interpretation of creation, sin and redemption in relation to gender, one which laid the basis for feminism and feminist theology that would begin to develop in the United States in the 1830s, significantly led by Quaker women, such as Sarah and Angelina Grimké, Lucretia Mott and Susan B. Anthony.[33] But it would take another century and a half before this reinterpreted understanding of the gospel and gender would emerge in a form that would challenge the public structures of church and state in the dominant society.

33. Schneir 1972: 76-82.

Chapter Four

The Development of the Egalitarian Paradigm in Modern Feminist Theology

As we have seen in the previous chapter, the egalitarian paradigm of gender in creation and redemption re-emerged in the humanist thinker Agrippa von Nettlesheim, and was developed by seventeenth-century Quakers in their theology of the church. But it was the marriage of radical Christianity and political liberalism that transformed this theological tradition into one that called for reform of women's legal status in society.

The eighteenth century saw a parallel development of two lines of Christian radical tradition. On the one hand, there were renewed mystical, millenarian communal movements that reclaimed the medieval tradition of Wisdom as the female expression of the divine. The most comprehensive expression of this tradition was the Shakers or Millennial Church of Christ's Second Appearing. The Shakers arose in England in the 1760s, drawing on several radical movements, including the Quakers. Under the leadership of Ann Lee, they moved to America in 1774, where they founded communal societies, remnants of which continue today.

The Shakers developed a comprehensive egalitarian model of theology and practice based on the belief that God is a dynamic unity of male and female, Power and Wisdom. Creation as male and female mirrors in nature this androgyny of God. Drawing on encratite themes from early Christianity, the Shakers taught that humans fell through the primal sin of the sexual act, and humanity will grow to its full redemptive maturity only through renunciation of sex for the celibate life. Redemption takes place through a four-stage dispensational history: first the patriarchal and Mosaic stages that teach humans moral discipline, then the manifestation of celibate redemption in the male line, Jesus Christ, and finally the culmination of redemption in the female line, in Mother Ann.[1] Redemption was incomplete in Jesus because there was not yet the power of the Holy Spirit to enable humans to rise to spiritual life. This spiritual power, disclosing the Wisdom side of God, is now revealed, expressed in the founding of the Millennial Church. The parallel aspects of God as male and female are reflected in church leadership in parallel pairs of male and female deacons and elders. The redemptive life is manifest in the Millennial Church through its practice of celibacy, renunciation of property for communal living, pacifism, rejecting all war and violence, and justice and harmony in human relations through restoring woman to her rightful place by the side of the male.

In the later nineteenth century Shakers identified with progressive movements, such as feminism, anti-racism, pacifism and socialism, and saw these movements as expressing a larger historical trajectory that would culminate in millennial peace and blessing. They interpreted their own movement as a seed planted that must die in order to give birth to this larger redemptive process in human history.[2] Many Shaker ideas reverberated in progressive American movements in the second half of the nineteenth century; divine androgyny that calls for a manifestation of the divine as female to complete the revelation of God and the redemption of humanity; communal living, justice between the sexes and races and peace as the expressions of redeemed human life. Many Americans shared their faith in progress as a redemptive process already planted in the present and leading surely to the Kingdom of God on earth in the near future.

Nineteenth-century feminist abolitionists, such as Sarah and Angelina Grimké, Lucretia Mott, Susan B. Anthony and Elizabeth Cady Stanton, represent a second line of feminist thought in which egalitarian Christianity is joined to political liberalism. Sarah and Angelina Grimké grew up as Presbyterians in a slave-owning family in South Carolina. Rejecting slavery, they moved to Philadelphia in the 1820s. They joined the Society of Friends, attracted by the Quaker views on anti-slavery and gender equality.[3] In the 1830s the Grimké sisters became activists in the Garrisonian wing of the abolitionist movement and began to publish

1.   The most comprehensive account of Shaker doctrine is found in the Shaker Bible (Youngs and Green 1856).

2.   For the Shaker embrace of pacifism and feminism, see White and Taylor (1904).

3.   See Lerner 1967.

tracts to defend their rejection of slavery. These were followed by writings on the equality of women, sparked by an attack by the Congregational clergy of Massachusetts, who claimed that the sisters' public preaching violated the order of creation and New Testament teaching that women must be subordinate to the male and silent in public.

The core of the sisters' argument against slavery and for equal rights for blacks and women rested on their reading of the Genesis teaching that all humans are created in the image of God. In their view this meant that humans of every race, male and female, are created equal and in possession of the same moral and intellectual nature, and so should be equal in rights and responsibilities in society. The power of some over others is not God's order of creation but the manifestation of human sinfulness. As Sarah Grimké put it, in her *Letters on the Equality of Women* in response to the Massachusetts clergy, 'The lust of domination was probably the first effect of the Fall, and as there was no other intelligent being over whom to exercise it, woman was the first victim of this unhallowed passion.'[4]

The mission of Christ was to restore the original equality of all humans in the image of God, overcoming the sinful systems of domination of male over female, master over slave. But the churches have betrayed this mission, creating new justifications of these evils. Far from violating divine law, the equality of women is no more than the restoration of God's original plan for human relations. In Grimké's words: 'But I ask no favors for my sex. I surrender not our claim to equality. All I ask of our brethren is that they will take their feet from off our necks and permit us to stand upright on the ground on which God has designed for us to occupy.'[5]

The marriage of Angelina Grimké to abolitionist leader Theodore Weld brought the retirement of the sisters from public life for domestic duties, but their work was continued by Lucretia Mott, Philadelphia Quaker minister, who united in her long career of religiously inspired activism the three causes of anti-slavery, anti-racism, feminism and peace.[6] Like the Grimkés, Lucretia Mott took her stand on a theology of original human nature as image of God. She identified this with her Quaker understanding of the inner light or the presence of the divine in the depths of each human person.

4.   See Ceplair 1989: 209.
5.   Ceplair 1989: 208.
6.   For a comprehensive biography of Mott, see Bacon (1980).

This divine presence manifests the true created nature of every human. It has not been lost in the Fall, although it has been distorted and silenced by ideologies and social systems of oppression, such as slavery, unjust luxury, racism, sexism and militarism. Christ came to disclose anew this divine nature of every human and to overcome such distorted systems of society, but the Christian clergy have betrayed his mission. Instead they have fashioned theologies of the Fall, imputed sin from Adam and Eve, human depravity and helplessness and the need of a Savior to dispense redeeming grace apart from any real moral action on our part, together with notions of the infallibility of Scripture and the need for external ceremonies for salvation, to fashion a system that justifies social evils and cautions Christians against any effort to transform society.

Mott set her face against such externalized 'do nothing' Christianity, which she saw as typical of the Protestant preaching of her day. In endless sermons and talks at women's rights, anti-slavery and peace meetings over 40 years she taught that our true spiritual and moral nature, manifesting God's presence within, is still our true self. Jesus is not other than, but himself simply an best exemplar of this true humanity in communion with the divine presence. It can and must be reawakened in us to become the basis for a life-long struggle to overcome both our personal lethargy and corruption and to join together to transform society from all the sinful systems of domination and to create a society where justice and peace will flourish.[7]

Together with Elizabeth Cady Stanton, Lucretia Mott convened the first Women's Rights' Convention in Seneca Falls, New York, in 1848. From this historic meeting was founded the women's suffrage movement that Stanton, soon joined by Susan B. Anthony, would lead for the next five decades. Mott would continue to appear at meetings of this movement until her death in 1880.

Neither Stanton nor Anthony would live to see the passage of the women's suffrage amendment in 1921, granting women legal equality before the law. But their successors, who led the women's suffrage movement to its successful conclusion, knew that the struggle for equal rights was hardly over with the passage of this amendment. Through the first elected congresswomen they placed before the American legislature the Equal Rights Amendment, designed to be a legal instrument to clear up continuing inequalities of women in legal codes and practices. They

7.   See Green 1980.

also founded the women's Peace Party, intended to carry out the larger dreams of women's suffrage as a means to ending war in international relations.

The Equal Rights Amendment struggled for passage for 50 years and finally was shot down by state legislatures in 1982. The statue of Mott, Anthony and Stanton donated to Congress by the Women's Party in 1921 to celebrate women's suffrage was quickly removed by Congressmen and put in a broom closet and later into the crypt of the Congress. Only after a long struggle was it restored to the Capitol rotunda in 1997, but without any inscription to explain what it represents.[8]

The Women's Party's commitment to world peace was silenced by the rise of fascism. From the Depression through the 1950s the vision of equality, justice and peace that inspired nineteenth-century Christian feminist movements was largely forgotten. The 1960s saw a reawakening of the struggle for racial justice, followed by the anti-war movement. Feminism too was reborn, and women began to re-examine their actual status 45 years after they had been declared 'equal.' In Western Europe too new movements for worker justice, women's rights and peace inspired waves of new radical movements. In Latin American, Asia and Africa struggles against neo-colonialism, poverty and Western military intervention inspired new revolutionary movements. An awareness of the costs of rapacious global industrialism on the bio-systems of the earth sparked the rise of the ecological movement.

These new movements for justice, peace and integrity of creation (to use the World Council of Churches language) would inspire waves of new theological reflection in the Christian churches; black theology, liberation theology, feminist theology, ecological theology. In North America and Western Europe the rise of feminist theology paralleled the rapid entrance of women into theological education and ordained ministry. Although a few American churches, the Congregationalists, Unitarians and Universalists began to ordain women in the 1850-80s, there was little further movement on this until the Methodist Episcopal and Presbyterian USA churches voted to ordain women in 1956.

In the following two decades most of American Protestantism would accept women's ordination. Similarly, in Europe the Lutheran and Reformed churches accepted women's ordination in the late 1950s and 1960s. Women began to enter theological education in Western Europe and North America in increasing numbers, today reflecting more than

8.   Ruether 1996a: 22.

half of theological students. The presence of increasing numbers of women in theological education from the mid-1960s brought a demand for women professors and for courses in all the theological disciplines, Bible, theology, ethics, church history, pastoral psychology and worship, from a feminist perspective.[9]

An extraordinary burst of creativity among women doctoral students, soon to be theological professors, has produced major studies in all these areas over the last 30 years. In 1972, when I taught my first course in theological history from a feminist perspective at Harvard Divinity School, I struggled to find any recent studies in this field. Today a bibliography of feminist studies across the fields of theological education would total thousands of books and articles.[10]

Nor is this work only being done by Euro-American women. Increasingly theologically educated African, Hispanic and Asian-American women are contextualizing theological reflection in their own cultural and social histories in America, shaping the distinct movements of Womanist, Mujerista and Asian-American feminist theology and ethics. Third World women also began to find their voices within the assemblies of Third World liberation theology. In 1982, at an assembly of the Ecumenical Association of Third World Theology in Geneva, African, Asian and Latin American women demanded their own women's association within this organization to contextualize their theologies.[11]

Third World women planned a process of national, regional and global gatherings over the next 15 years to shape feminist theologies in the many countries of Asia, Africa and Latin America. The writings of Third World feminist theologians, such as Chung Hyun Kyung, Mercy Oduyoye and Ivone Gebara[12] are becoming standard reading in feminist theology from a global perspective. Nor were Western European women inactive. Writers such as Dorothee Soelle in Germany, Kari Børresen in Scandinavia, Catharina Halkes in the Netherlands and Mary Grey in England[13] laid the foundations of feminist theology and for an

---

9. See Ruether 1994.

10. For example, the bibliography edited by Finson (1991), which has 207 pages, but only covers entries to 1990.

11. For the history of the Women's Commission of EATWOT, see Fabella (1993).

12. Major writings of these theologians are Kyung (1990a), Oduyoye (1995) and Gebara (1995).

13. Dorothy Soelle has many books and articles: for example, her *Theology for*

Association of European feminist theological researchers, which now gathers hundreds of scholars across Europe, increasingly joined by women from Eastern Europe.

Today in 1998 it can be truly said that Christian feminist theology is global. Nor have women from other religious traditions remained silent. Feminist theological reflection is also being shaped by Jewish, Buddhist, Muslim and Hindu women[14] as well. In the remainder of this essay, I will briefly delineate the key themes of of the understanding of redemption in these feminist theologies of North America, Western Europe and the so-called Third World (Latin America, Asia and Africa).

Contemporary feminist theologies reinvent the egalitarian anthropological paradigm of Christianity. Like the seventeenth-century Quakers and the abolitionist-feminists of the nineteenth century, they begin with the assumptions that woman is created equally in the image of God and that no subordination of woman to man is a part of 'original nature'. Feminism arises as the critique and rejection of any theological or sociobiological justification of women's subordination as valid due to some combination of natural inferiority, a divine mandate that women be subordinate in the order of creation and/or as punishment for a presumed priority in sin. Women's full and equal humanity with men and their right to equal access to education, professions and political participation in society are assumed.

The classical philosophical and Christian justifications of women's subordination as due to natural inferiority, subordination in creation and

---

Skeptics: Reflections on God (Soelle 1995). Kari Børresen's foundational book is *Subordination and Equivalence: The Nature and Role of Woman in Augustine and Thomas Aquinas*. This work was published in French in 1968 and in English in 1981 by the University Press of America. It has been reprinted with a new promotion by Kok Pharos in 1995. Catherine Halkes has few books or articles in English. A major one is her ecofeminist work, *New Creation: Christian Feminism and the Renewal of the Earth* (Halkes 1989). Mary Grey's major book is *Redeeming the Dream: Feminism, Redemption and Christian Tradition* (Grey 1989).

14.   The leading Jewish feminist theologian is Judith Plaskow (see Plaskow 1990). Rita Gross's *Buddhism after Patriarchy: A Feminist History, Analysis and Reconstruction of Buddhism* (Gross 1993), is the major feminist theology of Buddhism. Riffat Hassan is the best-known Muslim feminist theologian (see Hassan 1987: 2-4). Among Hindu feminists the best known is Vandana Shiva; see her *Staying Alive: Women, Ecology and Survival in India* (Shiva 1988). However Shiva is a scientist, not a scholar of Hinduism. For a critique of Shiva's use of Hinduism and a more developed effort to reconstruct Hinduism for ecofeminism, see Shema (1997).

punishment for sin are deprived of authority and discredited as false ideologies constructed by males to justify injustice. The domination of men over women is sinful, and patriarchy is a sinful social system. Far from reflecting the true will of God and the nature of women, such theological constructions subvert God's creation and distort the human nature of both men and women. Feminist theology is about the deconstruction of these ideological justifications of domination and the vindication of women's equality as the will of God, authentic human nature and Christ's redemptive intention. Redemption is about liberating women and all victimized people from violence and injustice.

Contemporary feminists did not know that earlier feminist forebears had already trodden these same paths, for these traditions had been marginalized in the dominant culture and were unknown to women who began to shape feminist theologies in the 1960s. Patriarchal power in society and culture not only subjugates women and other dominated groups, but erases the memory of alternative movements, socializing the next generation into a culture and memory of the past that justifies domination as normal, 'natural' and 'the way it has always been.'

This means that the egalitarian paradigm buried in early Christianity, as well as in subsequent Christian movements, has to be rediscovered as new feminist theologies arise and seek their historical precedents. The questioning of the ideologies of patriarchal theology itself leads to a quest that disinters the 'subversive memories' of buried past histories. We discover our Christian feminist ancestors as a second step that flows from a reawakened critical consciousness.

Contemporary feminist understanding of redemption follows a modern western cultural shift from individualistic and otherworldly to social and this worldly hope. This shift is itself a recovery of the social, historical understanding of redemption of the biblical tradition, as we saw in the beginning of Chapter 1. Platonizing Christianity made redemption individualistic and otherworldly. Redemption came to be seen primarily as being reconciled with God, from whom our human nature is seen as having become totally severed due to sin, rejecting our bodies and finitude and ascending to communion with a heavenly world that is to be our true home after death.

The social historical approach also is rooted in a positive understanding of God's continuing relation to creation. Redemption is about reclaiming an original goodness as image of God that is still available as our true selves, although it has been obscured by unjust social structures that give unjust power to some at the expense of others and by false ideologies that wish to socialize us all to accept this.

Redemption puts us back in touch with the full biophilic relationality of humans with our bodies, with one another and with the earth and rebuilds social relations that can incarnate justice and love. Thus redemption is about the transformation of self and society into good, life-giving relations, rather than escape from the body and the world into eternal life. Otherworldly eschatology is not necessarily denied, but it is put aside as the focus of attention and understanding of redemption.

Contemporary feminist theologies in North America, Western Europe and the so-called 'Third World' are engaged in in-depth explorations of the many aspects of this re-envisioned understanding of human nature, as male and female, sin and redemption. This involves a detailed critique of how the false ideologies that sacralize patriarchy have been constructed in different branches of Christianity and in different social and cultural contexts. It also involves a quest for positive resources for reconstructing an alternative view of God, humanity, male and female, nature and society to ground a vision of reconciliation with one another, the earth and with God. Feminist theologies arise in many distinct contexts, Euro-American, African-American, Asian, African and Latin America, to pose these questions in their distinct social histories and cultures.

These explorations leave open many disputed questions. One of these is the relation of the concept of 'human nature' to gender difference, male and female. Feminist theology and theory has long struggled to reconcile a one-nature and a two-nature anthropology of gender. The one-nature anthropology is rooted in the Christian idea of an original asexual image of God given equally to all humans in creation. It assumes that all humans have the 'same' human nature. Modern liberalism reclaimed this tradition as the basis for its political theory that 'all men are created equal, and endowed by their creator with certain inalienable rights', while denying these rights to women, slaves and other dependent people.

The problem with this one-nature anthropology is that it has been implicitly androcentric. Essential human nature is identified with such qualities as reason and moral will, linked to males and assumed to be deficient in females *qua* female. The covert androcentrism of one-nature anthropology has the result of either denying that women are included in this 'essential humanity', at least in its full and normative form, or else including women only by negating their femaleness.

Two-nature anthropology, by contrast, makes male and female difference essential. Maleness and femaleness are seen as equally good, but totally different or 'opposite'. The fullness of humanity exists only in the complementary relation of the two with each other. The anthropology of complementarity draws on sophiological and mariological traditions of the 'good feminine'. Women are called to exemplify this good femininity associated with altruistic love and service to 'others', that is, men and children, in a way that re-enforces women's passive, auxiliary relation to male agency. Maleness continues to be identified with reason and moral will, complemented by female intuitive and altruistic qualities. While often exalting women as 'naturally' more virtuous than men, two-nature anthropology excludes women from being autonomous persons and active moral agents in their own right.[15]

Feminists have sought to transcend the dilemma that puts them in a double bind between an androcentric one-nature and a complementarian two-nature anthropology. They have reached for an enlarged understanding of the human that unites all the qualities split into male and female into a transformed whole, calling women and men into journeys of growth into wholeness by which each can reclaim the repressed parts of themselves that have been assigned to the opposite gender. Men need to combine gentleness and caring with strength and rationality, and women to integrate rationality and strength into caring and compassion for others. Yet the questions of how women are different from men, while at the same time being 'equal', possessing the same humanness as the basis for equal rights in society, continues to plague feminist anthropology.[16]

In the last two decades of the twentieth century this discussion of what a holistic humanness in mutual relation would mean for transformed women and men in a good society has been challenged by postmodernist thought and also by the rise of new voices of women from non-white and non-Western cultures. Post-modernism has rejected the whole idea of universals, not only of essential maleness and essential femaleness, but also of essential humanness.

All ideas of an essential human self and universal values are declared social constructions that veil the cultural imperialism of dominant groups of western men and women. We need to accept a normless

15. See the discussion in Ruether 1983: 102-109.
16. Ruether 1983:109-15.

infinite particularity. There is no generic, essential 'woman's experience' that can be used as a basis of feminist critique of patriarchy or sisterhood of women across cultures.[17]

The emergence of new voices of women from African-American, Hispanic, Asian, African and Latin American contexts has also challenged the tendencies of some earlier feminist theory and theology done by white women to ignore their own ethnic and class contexts. These women of 'color' in America and the Third World are defining their theologies in their own historical and cultural contexts. But generally these women are not interested in the post-modern emphasis on an endless difference that ends in impenetrable and normless particularity. Rather they wish to establish their own distinct contexts and experiences as women in order to construct new and more authentic ways of reaching across these differences to solidarity in struggle against systems of oppression that are both particular and global.

Increasingly feminist theology has recognized that the affirmation of women as equal in creation and redemption means more than just adding female symbols to an unchanged hierarchical cosmology. Overcoming patriarchal theology means dismantling the entire cosmovision based on a dualistic universe in which God is located in a disembodied mental realm outside of and ruling over the bodily universe. Redemption does not mean sending the divine 'down' from the higher spiritual world in which God is located to a bodily world defined as alien to God, but rather the welling up of authentic life in and through creation, transforming us from death-dealing to life-giving relations.

Spirit and matter, God and body, need to be reintegrated, locating God as the source of renewal of loving, life-giving interaction in mutual relations. God is not the power of dominating control from outside, but the matrix or ground of life-giving relations and their ongoing renewal. Carter Heyward particularly has worked on the deconstruction of the dualistic hierarchical cosmovision, reconstructing the understanding of God in relation to us as the ground of transformative mutuality.[18]

Feminist theology also dismantles a Christology based on both a masculinist concept of God and a masculinist idea of authentic humanity. Such a Christology means that women can never 'image Christ' since they cannot image either the male God or the masculine humanity of Christ. This argument has been key to the Catholic and Orthodox claim

17. For the feminist discussion of post-modernism, see Nicolson 1990.
18. See, for example, Heyward 1982, 1989.

that women cannot be ordained since they cannot, as women, 'image Christ'. But the argument overshoots its mark, since it also assumes that women cannot image God and hence lack the image of God. Ultimately it throws in question whether women are indeed redeemed by a Christ who represents both a God and a human nature that excludes women.[19]

Feminist theology dismantles this masculinist Christology by reclaiming the iconoclastic Jesus of the Gospels, the Jesus who overturns patriarchal religious and social hierarchy, who preaches good news to the poor, the liberation of the captive and takes the side of the victims in society, including despised women. This Jesus is seen, not only as an advocate of women and other despised people, but as entering their condition, suffering with them, becoming victimized by the same system that despises and victimizes them. As one who stands with them and suffers as they suffer, Jesus is the redeemer of women.

Yet this emphasis on Jesus as co-sufferer with women and other oppressed people also raises the question of the role of suffering and the cross in redemption. What kind of suffering is redemptive? Is the passive suffering of victims redemptive? Does the mandate that women and other victims, such as slaves, accept suffering in order to be Christlike not simply prolong and justify violence, rather than overcome it?

Some theologians, such as womanist Delores Williams, have answered this question by a decisive rejection of the idea of the cross or Christ's suffering as redemptive. It is not Jesus' suffering and death, but his life as a praxis of protest against injustice and solidarity in defense of life that is redemptive. We need to imitate Jesus, not by acquiescence to being crucified, which represents the victory of oppressors who sought to silence him, but in his protest against evil and his defense of life.[20]

Suffering is a factor in the redemptive process, not as a means of redemption, but as the risk that Jesus took and that we take when confronting and denouncing unjust systems whose beneficiaries resist change. But the efficacious means and process of redemption is not more victimization, but conversion, the changing of persons and systems from violence and injustice to loving and life-giving relations.

Although the figure of Jesus remains resiliently central for Christian feminist theology, many Christian feminists would also reject a christological exclusivism. The Jesus who takes the side of the poor, who

19. See Rosemary Ruether's 'The Redemption of Christology from Patriarchy' and other essays in Stevens (1993).
20. Williams 1993a.

celebrates life with the marginalized, is key to the feminist paradigm of redemptive process, but this does not exclude, but rather embraces parallel paradigms in women's experience and in other cultures and religious traditions. Thus Chung Hyun Kyung, Korean feminist theologian, embraces symbols from shamanism and Buddhism in union with Christian ecofeminism;[21] African feminist Mercy Oduyoye embraces African liberating symbols together with those from Christianity[22] and Mexican feminist Elsa Tamez parallels Christ with the Natuatl god-man Quetzalcoatl.[23]

This practice of multi-religious resourcing is emerging not only as acceptable but as required for a feminist theology done by women whose historical religious cultures are plural, and who cannot affirm their own wholeness apart from embracing this cultural plurality. Thus feminist liberation theology in its increasingly plural forms opens up as an inclusively human project, not only a Christian project, but also not less a Christian project. Feminist theology thus reaches back to the egalitarian paradigm of early prophetic Christianity, but it also expands forward into an embrace of liberating paradigms across human cultures and histories, pointing toward a still unrealized hope for the reign of God's shalom on earth.

21. Chung Hyun Kyung's plenary address at the World Council of Churches 7th Assembly in Canberra, Australia, 'Come Holy Spirit: Renew the Whole Creation', best illustrates her synthesis of her religious traditions. The video of this talk is available from Lou Niznik, 15726 Ashland Drive, Laurel, MD 20707, USA.

22. See Oduyoye and Amoah 1988: 35-36.

23. Tamez 1992.

Chapter Five

Feminist Metanoia and Soul-Making: The Journey of Conversion in Feminist Perspective

In this chapter I explore feminist metanoia and soul-making, that is, the journey of conversion and transformation toward self-realization in relation to gender socialization. The word feminist, in this context, means not simply a political analysis and social change of patriarchal systems, although it is surely that, but how feminism calls both women and men into personal and social conversion and transformation. I begin by saying something about how I understand patriarchy and other systems of domination as sin, creating alienation and oppression in different ways for women and for men.

Classical Christianity has seen 'sin' as a condition of alienation from God, rooted in a primordial 'fall', which we inherit biologically. The possibility of being rescued from this alienation from God has been laid through the sacrifice of Christ, but we have to include ourselves or be included in that saving event through baptism and personal experience of conversion. We can then grow in grace through being incorporated into this new life in Christ. This is the traditional Christian prescription for 'soul-making'.

My view of sin and conversion differs from this classical view. I view human capacities as ambivalent rather than depraved or in an irreparable condition of alienation. I prefer the traditional Jewish concept of the 'two tendencies', the tendency to good and the tendency to evil, and believe that we retain the capacity to choose between them.[1] I also see

---

1. Judaism does not accept the Christian idea of 'original sin', but speaks instead of humans as possessing 'two tendencies', the tendency to good and the tendency to evil. It exhorted humans to choose good and avoid evil, with the belief that humans had the free will to do so. This same concept of the two tendencies or 'two ways' is

the good tendency as that which connects us to our authentic existence, our true 'nature', our 'imago Dei'. But I also agree with the view, found somewhat in Judaism, but developed in Christianity, that our tendency to evil has been biased by historical systems of evil.[2]

The world into which we are born is not neutral, but has been deeply distorted on the side of alienation and violence. We are socialized from infancy to conform to those systems, as if they were normal, natural and the will of God. Thus in order to find the right path to spiritual health, we not only have to confront our own sadistic and masochistic tendencies, but also have to unmask the claims of the dominant culture that misleads us about the nature of good and evil. This can mean struggling against persons and institutions, such as family, school, church and country, that are close to us, that call for our allegiance and will be somewhere between disappointed and hostile to us if we choose a dissenting path.

My understanding of what sin is does not begin with the concept of alienation from God, a concept that strikes me as either meaningless or highly misleading to most people today. I think we need to start with alienation from one another. We can then go on to understand how alienation from one another expresses itself in personal relations and social relations of negation of others, as well as self-negation, that are sick-making and violent.

We can then look at the larger systems of social power and culture that re-enforce these patterns. Today we have to understand such patterns of destructivity not only in terms of society, but also in relation to the sustaining environment of nature. Patterns of injustice not only destroy society, they also devastate the earth. It is in this expanded understanding of alienation that we might begin to grasp anew what alienation from God might mean, that is to say, alienation from the very source and sustaining matrix of life itself.

also found in second-century Christian literature, rooted in this Jewish tradition, for example, the Didache and the Epistle of Barnabas. See Kraft 1965: 4–16.

2.   The idea that the Fall does not corrupt human free will, but biases the social world toward evil, which then socializes us into this bias, but one from which we can extricate ourselves by the exercise of will and the cultivation of good habits, was particularly developed by Pelagius, who was vehemently attacked for this view by Augustine. For Pelagius's view, see Burns (1981: 39–56). In the late nineteenth century Walter Rauschenbusch developed a social view of the transmission of sin to say that society, not biology, transmits sin. See Rauschbusch 1918.

Christians have for too long mixed up the concept of evil as sin with problems of finitude and mortality.[3] Natural limitations should be seen as sources of tragedy, but not the result of sin.[4] What is appropriately called sin belongs to that sphere of human freedom where we have the possibility of enhancing life or stifling it. When this freedom is misused, patterns and organizational systems of relationship are generated where competitive hatred builds up. This violence is sustained both by the egoistic refusal of mutuality, but also by passive acquiescence to victimization of others or of ourselves.

The central issue of sin as distinct from finitude, as I see it, is the misuse of freedom to exploit humans and other earth creatures and thus to violate the basic relations that sustain life; physically, psychically and spiritually. Life is sustained by a biotic relationality in which the whole attains well-being through mutually affirming interdependency. This is a fancy way of saying that life is sustained by love. When one part of any relationship exalts itself at the expense of other parts, life is diminished for these others. Ultimately the exploiters also diminish the quality of their own life as well, although material profit may abound for them. An expanding cycle of violence is generated.

Sin as distorted relationship has three dimensions: there is a personal-interpersonal dimension, a social-historical dimension and an ideological-cultural dimension. It is imperative to give due recognition to all three dimensions, and not only to focus on the personal-interpersonal aspect, as our confessional and therapeutic traditions have generally done.

On the interpersonal level, sin is the distortion of relationship, by which some persons absolutize their rights to life and potency at the expense of others with whom they are interdependent. Thus, for example, in male–female relations men were exalted as those persons in the family system with the superior right to be valued, to receive education in preparation for gainful economic roles and political participation in society. Women were accordingly disvalued. They were denied these

3.   The notion that death is not natural but the result of the fall into sin, the original created humans being undying, was assumed in the fourth-century Church Fathers, such as Gregory Nyssa and Augustine, and continued to be accepted by medieval and Reformation theology: see Chapters 2 and 3 above.

4.   Kathleen Sands has particularly developed the argument that feminist theologians have focused too much on sin or culpable evil and not enough on tragedy: see Sands 1994.

advantages of self-development in order to function as auxiliaries to male development.

Christianity was not entirely wrong in seeing the heart of sin as pride, an egoistic selfishness that reduces all others to objectified instrumentality. But it has defined this wrong relationship primarily vis-à-vis God, and thus failed to develop the implications of this teaching for relations to other people. Although pride is certainly an element in distorted relationship, I suggest that this is an unhelpful beginning point, particularly for women and for those men who have primarily been on the underside of systems of privilege. But even for those men who appear fairly advantaged, issues of insecurity and fear of vulnerability need to be recognized.

What is called pride, not to be confused with healthy self-esteem, is generally a cover-up for deep-seated dis-ease with oneself. Moreover, the prideful claims of superiority and privilege of some persons and groups over others can only be maintained by some combination of coercive repression and co-optation of these others. In one way or another one must force the victims to acquiesce to and even become collaborators in their own victimization. Aggressive pride can abound only when fed by passive acquiescence of others, and the ability to isolate enemies who can be violently coerced into subjugation. One has to see all these elements of the pathological relationship.

Some of the earlier ventures of feminist ethics suggested that women's sins are primarily the sins of passivity, of failure to develop an autonomous self, leaving in place the assumption that men sin primarily through pride. Naming passivity as well as pride as components of sin was a significant advance in ethical understanding of the pathological distortion of relationship, but dividing it neatly by gender is too simple.[5]

Although women have been directed to accept passivity, acquiescence and auxiliary existence to men as 'feminine virtue', they also exist within class and race hierarchies where they can exercise exploitative hauteur toward those under their power. Women, as well as men, in 'advisory' relations, also learn to cultivate passive aggressive or manipulative use of power to control those whom they cannot dominate directly.

Patriarchal masculinity has directed men to develop a self-confident,

---

5.   This feminist critique of the sin of pride was first developed by Valerie Saiving Goldstein (1960: 110-12). Judith Plaskow developed and applied this thesis to the study of Reinhold Niebhur and Paul Tillich, in her doctoral thesis (Plaskow 1980).

in-charge relationship to women and others under their power, but such confidence does not come easily. The appearance of confident control covers over insecurity. The deeper this insecurity the more it generates a cycle of violence. The male growing to manhood in patriarchal society was parented as a child largely by women. His masculinity is rooted in the overthrow of the mother who was once the all-powerful presence in his early life.

Thus, I suggest, underneath every assertion of male hegemony over women is the fear of women as the 'great mother'. The more insecure his 'manhood', the more aggressively he needs to put down his wife in order to secure his emancipation from his mother. The need for totally secure, dominating power characteristic of egoistic aggression feeds on an unsatisfied void of an insecure, ungrounded self, with its unresolved fears of vulnerability and dependency.

Although the roots of domination in the insecure self is most obvious in gender relations, it lies at the heart of every dominating and exploita-tive relationship. White racists need continually to repress blacks and punish them for the first signs of 'uppityness'. Anti-Semitic Christians needed to repress and punish Jews in order to secure their claims to be God's new 'chosen people'. Right-wing Israeli Jews need continually to silence Palestinians and to punish their smallest self-expression in order to maintain the claim that the land of Palestine is theirs and theirs ex-clusively. The militarist needs enemies who justify his demands for ever larger and more total systems of military might.

This cycle of violence is fed by the belief that, if more and more power is gained over the subjugated other, the possibility that they might threaten one's own power will finally be crushed. The other as other will be eliminated altogether, or reshaped as a totally docile in-strument of benefit to oneself. But this can never be accomplished, both because the dominating relationship eventually prompts rebellion from the dominated, but also because the dominator himself can only be a dominator through the existence of enemies to be vanquished. This became evident with the recent end of the cold war, where we saw the scramble of the US government military-industrial complex to identify new enemies to justify their arsenals.

But the patterns of domination are not created *de novo* in the move-ment of privileged males from the nursery to the playing fields to the killing fields. Rather these familial patterns are themselves kept in place and re-enforced by the larger historical, social structures in which the family is embedded as a dependent part. We are born into this system of patriarchal relations. We are socialized to accept our roles within it, as males or females, as members of more or less privileged class and racial groups, as if it were normal, natural and the will of God.

This is the inherited, collective, historical dimension of sin, which Christianity called 'original sin', mistakenly seeing its inheritability as the fruit of sexual reproduction, rather than the historical reproduction of social relations. This is also where sin is experienced as unfreedom, as a power that defines and controls us and that we feel powerless to change, even when we become aware of it as wrong.

We are born into sexist, racist, classist, militarist systems of society. This has shaped who we are from birth, and even before birth, for privilege and unprivilege mean that children may be well or badly nurtured even in the womb owing to the availability or lack thereof of good food and medical care for their mothers. Distorted, exploitative relationships are embedded in legal, economic and political systems that define the world around us. This is what the biblical tradition calls 'the powers and principalities'.

Exploitative social systems are also maintained and reproduced through ideologies that make themselves the hegemonic culture. It is the purpose of this hegemonic culture to make such unjust relationships appear good, natural, inevitable and even divinely mandated. To question or rebel against such relationships is to rebel against nature and nature's God. Family, school, church, media are all enlisted to socialize both the privileged and the disprivileged to accept their place and role in this system of evil, to interiorize its mandates as their identity and duty.

Yet we are not left without a trace of our '*imago Dei*', of our capacity for healthy and life-giving relationality, intimations of which persist in our intuitive sensibilities despite this ideological and social misshaping. Nor are we left without exemplars of good and life-giving relationships in family, friends, mentors in education, religion, work and even sometimes in politics. We inherit critical counter-cultures and communities, the fruit of past transforming movements in society, that hold forth alternative visions.

Culture and society, then, also express the struggle between the 'two tendencies', the tendency to just and loving relations and the tendency to hostile negation and exploitation of others and of ourselves. How then do we understand growth in the 'good tendency', or 'soul-making'? We might describe this as the process of enhancing our capacities, both personally and socially, for sustaining just and loving relationality, of curbing and curing fear of and contempt for others and for ourselves.

Soul-making does not lie in splitting our minds from our bodies, our reason from our passions, as though our good tendency lay in our rationality and our bad tendency in our bodies and passions. Nor can we just turn the dualism upside down, trusting impulse and rejecting thought. We need to look at this process holistically. Soul-making happens through transformative metanoia, which is both sudden insight and also slow maturation of a grounded self in relationship or community, able to be both self-affirming and other-affirming in life-enhancing mutuality. It is both a gift and a task, grace and work.

Such transformative metanoia is both personal and social. It cannot be fulfilled simply as an individual journey, although some individuals seem to accomplish a remarkable depth of soul; of inward tranquility and kindness to others in the midst of hostile relationships. As sin is not a 'something', a bad 'part' of ourselves, but distorted relationship, so metanoia or soul-making is essentially a journey of transformed relationship, relationship to oneself, to one's immediate community, of society and of culture, finally, a transformation of our relationship to all creation, to animals and plants, air, soil and water. Reconciliation with God is within this whole process of transformation and reconciliation with others. It is what the biblical tradition calls the 'reign of God'.

Our journeys of metanoia and soul-making will differ both because of the differences of individual histories and because of differences of social context, as males or females, as white, black, Asian, or other ethnic cultures, as more or less privileged economically. Women within the same general class and culture differ in the extent to which they have been socialized to accept patriarchal mores and abused by its violence. Similarly patriarchal self-identity has 'taken' with some men more deeply than with others. Family patterns, social environment, as well as differences in 'temperament' that cannot easily be explained by socialization, all play a role in these differences.

To the extent to which these patriarchal patterns have been held lightly, with positive role models of mutuality available, the journey may seem easy or obvious, while the abused woman who has internalized patriarchal sanctions may experience its discrediting as deeply traumatic. She may be precipitated out of its securities only through profound outer crisis in which remaking her inner world becomes necessary for her own personal survival. Some kind of alternative community that provides an alternative culture and world view also is essential for her to embark on this journey.

A woman who experiences dissenting thoughts alone, without any network of communication to support her, can hardly bring such dissent to consciousness. She is cowed into submission by the authorities of family, school, church, etc. that surround her and judge that such dissent is the sign of either sin or craziness or both. Thus only when there is a feminist movement that has been able to establish some foothold, creating an alternative vision of being a woman, developing networks of communication and community, can critical and transformative feminist self-perception come to consciousness and be acted upon in a woman's life. The consciousness-raising groups of 1960s feminism were examples of such communities.

Openness to feminist consciousness demands that the ideology and socialization into 'feminine virtue' be thrown into question. All the ways that women have been taught to be 'pleasing' and 'acceptable' to men are critically reviewed as possible tools of false consciousness and seduction, preventing women from asking who they are as persons. Although feminist parents may try to raise daughters and sons to be egalitarian, it is not easy for individual families to compete with the larger culture. Teenage and young adult years are a time of strong needs to conform to the peer group and its social references. Thus the deeper journey out of patriarchal consciousness often is one that belongs more to the mature stage of life.

Yet if women comply with traditional female roles well into their adult years, and receive some status and secondary power through this compliance, it also becomes difficult to make this journey. Such women have lost a large part of their lives. They have missed the educational opportunities to develop skills for a more self-defined life. It is painful to face up to their own self-betrayal, as well as betrayal by those with whom they have identified themselves. Such women become ready candidates for anti-feminist crusades.

For Christian women from conservative traditions one of the most difficult barriers to feminist consciousness is the Christian identification of sin with pride and anger and virtue with humility and self-abnegation. They have been told they must always put others, their parents, husband, children, first. For women this view of sin and virtue functions as a powerful re-enforcement of female subjugation and lack of self-esteem.[6] Such women feel that rebellious thoughts and self-affirmation are the roots of that sin of Eve for which they must atone by redoubled self-negation, even accepting abuse as the means of salvation. Women are to become 'Christlike' by having no self of their own. They will save themselves and their abusers by accepting exploitation and becoming 'suffering servants'.[7]

In the context of such socialization, the claiming of one's own quest for selfhood seems forbidden territory. Yet the conditions that precipitate such a choice for one's own personhood may be experienced, not only as traumatic, but also as exhilarating. In the classical Christian sense of conversion as an experience of transforming grace from beyond our present reality, conversion from sexism is like a gift of power and expanded possibilities.

Part of this breakthrough experience also involves getting in touch with one's own anger and hurt, bringing to consciousness one's experiences of betrayal and abuse and recognizing one's own complicity with this diminishment. This anger also has an energizing element, like a new inner power that allows one to break the chains that have bound one to the culture and systems of sexism.

Consciousness of this personal history also leads to recognition of the collective history of patriarchy and its stratagems of enforcing female subjugation. One begins to read, and perhaps write, this collective history in all of its ramifications. One's anger deepens as the fuller collective history comes into view. One should not short-circuit this work of anger, but also one must recognize its dangers, the danger of being stuck in soul-destroying resentment. Thus the unleashing of consciousness of all that has been lost and destroyed needs to become deeply rooted in love, self-love and compassion for others. One needs to move through anger to a deep enough self-esteem to forgive oneself and one's victimizers. To forgive, however, is not to forget, or to capitulate once again into victimization. It is only from a context of a certain confident autonomy, one that also allows some critical distance on one's own capacities to oppress others, that one can rebuild relations with others and with oneself, moving into increased capacity for mutuality.

Such a journey cannot remain only on the personal/interpersonal level, nor can it develop simply as consciousness without praxis. It needs

6.   See, for example, Welter 1976.
7.   For a critique of the way the theology of Christ's suffering lends itself to the justification of domestic violence, see the essays in Brown and Bohn (1989).

to be actualized in action. A woman may decide to seek additional education in preparation for new arenas of life. In so doing relations with
significant others will be transformed, or perhaps broken. In the process
new awareness of the workings of the structures and ideology of patriarchy comes to be recognized.

But the journey of feminist soul-making must also break out beyond
the boundaries of the personal journey and become a journey in solidarity with others, others of one's own group and also others across class
and race. This recognition that one's own liberation is an integral part of
the liberation of a community, a people, comes much more readily to
women of oppressed races and groups. The ideological and cultural en-
capsulation of middle-class white people, women as well as men, make
it much more difficult to see beyond the personal/interpersonal arena.

Yet, as women seeking liberation enter into this larger struggle for
liberation, they also recognize more fully who they are. When a woman
is a person of some class and race privilege, she must also take account of
her own capacity to victimize others or simply to be the unconscious
recipient of benefits based on their exploitation. One becomes more
aware of the ways that the victim too learns to victimize others. This
critical distance on one's own context, however, must also become a
committed and compassionate praxis, a praxis of solidarity that seeks to
ameliorate the systems of exploitation that perpetuate the cycle of violence.

Parallel to the female journey into liberation from patriarchy there
also needs to be a male journey. I do not attempt to chart its process
here. The fuller description of its dynamics awaits a mature men's
movement. Much of what is passing for 'the men's movement' at the
moment does not yet seem to me to qualify for such a mature movement of men against patriarchy, but has many features of reduplication
of male patriarchal identities and relationships.[8]

A mature men's movement can only arise among men who have been
willing to listen to women's story long enough to care deeply about
what has happened to women under patriarchy, to have become compassionate enough to support women's journey into an autonomy that
can allow genuine peer relations between men and women, and also
courageous enough to risk ridicule and censure from other men when
one breaks with patriarchal sanctions. A mature men's movement would
also recognize that it has to move beyond the personal/interpersonal

8.   See the essays in Hagan 1992.

context toward a struggle for transformation of the larger social structures of injustice.[9]

The journey of 'soul-making' is incomplete without a transformation of the whole. To adapt Augustine's language, our hearts are restless until we rest in this whole.[10] Unlike Augustine, however, we cannot split reconciliation with God from reconciliation with all the others with whom we are interdependent. Indeed our hearts must remain restless, and stir up restlessness anew, as long as women are raped, children beaten, men sent to war, animals are tortured to make them our meat. To remain in compassionate relation to all others who suffer is not simply a gracious choice of the saint, but a necessity of our reality. To 'bliss-out' by oneself in the midst of a suffering world is denial of one's own reality, one's interdependency and complicity with this suffering.

Yet, since total transformation and reconciliation will never be fully accomplished within history, since the reign of God is an eschatological norm, not a historical possibility, since both tragedy and sin will continue, hopefully partially alleviated by our struggles for personal and social metanoia, we also have to learn to sustain our soul-making in our personal and social relationships in the midst of defeat. We have to taste wholeness in the midst of the insufficiencies and tragedies of natural life, of the child born brain-damaged, the young man inexplicably stricken down by disease in the prime of life. We also have to sustain our faith, hope and capacity for love in the midst of cruel reversals of our best efforts, victories betrayed and the martyrdom of prophets.

Soul-making takes place in and through the cross, yet in spite of the cross. The cross is not our goal. Christians must cure themselves of a masochistic spirituality that glories in suffering, usually prescribing it as a way of perfection to be endured by those already victimized. Natural suffering, or tragedy, and unnatural suffering, or unjust violence, are neither the goal nor the way of soul-making, but they are the context in which we must endure and keep the faith in healing love, despite the presence of its contradictions.

The journey of soul-making in community is a never completed or perfected process. There will be no millennium where it is established 'once-and-for-all' in static perfection. Rather we must take up the task in each day, in each relationship, in each generation, in specific social

9.   For a discussion of a genuinely pro-feminist men's movement, see the essay by Margo Adair in Hagan (1992: 63-66).

10.   Augustine, *Confessions* 1.1.

and historical contexts; the struggle to enhance loving, truthful and just relationships and to curb and cure hate, fear and violence. It is in this way that we also both receive and manifest the redemptive work of the Holy One.

Chapter Six

Can a Male Savior Save Women?
Liberating Christology from Patriarchy

In Vatican and Roman Catholic episcopal statements Christology has been used as the keystone of the argument against women's ordination. It is said that women, by their very nature, cannot 'image' Christ. Therefore they cannot be priests, since priests 'represent' Christ.[1] This argument has been echoed in other high church statements, Anglican, Lutheran and Eastern Orthodox. What is the meaning of this use of Christology against women's full participation in the Christian church? If women cannot represent Christ, in what sense can it be said that Christ represents women? Does this not mean that Christ does not redeem women, but re-enforces women's bondage in a patriarchal social system? If this is the case, should women who seek liberation from patriarchy not reject Christianity?

It has traditionally been claimed that Christ is the redeemer and representative of all humanity. He is the one who overcomes that bondage to sin that is the universal human dilemma. Thus it would seem that the symbols that the Christian church uses to express Christology should manifest a like universality and inclusivity. These symbols should embrace the authentic humanness and fulfilled hopes of all persons. How is it possible that more than half of humanity, more than half of the members of Christian churches themselves, find themselves inferiorized and excluded by Christology?

---

1.   This argument that women cannot be ordained because they do not image Christ is found in the 'Vatican Declaration on the Question of the Admission of Women to the Ministerial Priesthood' (1976), sec. 27. The argument was repeated in the pastoral letter by Pope John Paul II, 'The Dignity and Vocation of Women', 31 September 1988, sec. 26, and in the pastoral on women by the American Catholic bishops, 'One in Christ: A Pastoral Response to the Concerns of Women for Church and Society' (second draft), *Origins*, 5 April 1990, sec. 115, p. 730.

In this chapter I will examine the development of the christological symbols and how they have been shaped by an androcentric ideology that becomes explicit when they are used to exclude women from representation of Christ. I will then ask whether Christology can be liberated from this androcentric bias and become genuinely inclusive of women?

Early Christianity used the word 'Logos' to define that presence of God made incarnate in Jesus the Christ. This term drew on a long tradition of religious philosophy. In Greek and Hellenistic Jewish philosophy, the divine Logos was the means by which the transcendent God came forth in the beginning to shape the visible cosmos. The Logos was simultaneously the immanence of God and the ground of the visible cosmos. In Hellenistic Jewish terms, the Logos, or Sophia (Wisdom), was God's self-manifestation by which God created the world, providentially guided it, was revealed to it and through whom the world was reconciled to God. The Logos was particularly identified with the rational principle in each human soul. By linking the term Christ (Messiah), through whom God redeemed the world, to the Logos, as the creational principle, early Christianity prevented a split between redemption and creation threatened by gnosticism. Christians affirmed that the God revealed in Jesus Christ was the same God who created the world in the beginning. Christ was the authentic ground of creation, manifest in fulfilled form, over against the alienation of creation from its true being. This concept of the Logos as the divine identity of Christ would seem to be inclusive of women, pointing all humans, male and female, to the foundation of their true humanness.[2]

But this Hellenistic philosophical tradition was also shaped in a patriarchal culture that gave the terms Logos and Christ an androcentric bias. Since divinity, sovereign power, rationality and normative humanity were assumed to be male, the theological points of reference for defining Christ were defined in male terms. Normative humanity, the image of God in 'man' and the divine Logos became interlocking androcentric concepts in the theological definition of Christ, re-enforcing the assumption that God is male and that the human Christ must be a male in order to reveal the male God.

Christianity has never said that God was literally male, but it has

<hr>

2.   For the development of Logos Christology in the New Testament, especially in the Gospel of John, see Dodd (1963: 263-85). For its development in the second century, see Goodenough (1968: 139-75).

assumed that God represents pre-eminently the qualities of rationality and sovereign power. Since it is men that were assumed to be rational, and women less so or not at all, and men who exercised public power, normally denied to women, the male metaphor was seen as appropriate for God, while female metaphors for God came to be regarded as inappropriate and even 'pagan'. The Logos who reveals the 'Father' was presumed to be properly imaged as male, even though the Jewish Wisdom tradition had used the female metaphor, Sophia, for this same idea. The maleness of the historical Jesus re-enforced this preference for male-identified metaphors, such as Logos and 'Son of God', over the female metaphor of Sophia.

In Trinitarian theology, the use of the word 'Son' for the Logos or second person of the Trinity is misleading, since it suggests a subordinate and derivative status of the Logos, as the male child is 'begotten' by and under the power of his Father. This 'Son-Father' metaphor is used to represent the immanence of God as 'under' and derivative from divine transcendence. Taken literally, these metaphors re-enforce the maleness of God, and set up a patriarchal relationship between the two 'male persons' of God.

These notions of the maleness of God also affect the interpretation of the concept of *imago Dei*. Genesis 1.27-28 says, 'So God created man [Adam] in his own image, in the image of God he created him, male and female he [they] created them.' This formula, with its plural, collective term for God, leaves open the possibility that the human thus created is to be understood generically, and that Genesis 1.27b teaches that the image of God is possessed by both male and female. This would mean that woman shares in the stewardship over creation referred to in Gen. 1.26.[3]

However, most of the patristic and medieval tradition rejected the possibility that women *qua* female were equally theomorphic.[4] In most interpretations the concept of *imago Dei* was distinguished from gender difference. One way to interpret this distinction was to make the *imago Dei* asexually spiritual, and so neither male nor female. Gender difference would then be referred to the bodily characteristics that humans share with animals but not with God. Following Philo, some Church

---

3. For a critical exegesis of this passage, see Bird (1981).

4. For essays on the historical development of the exclusion and gradual inclusion of women as *imago Dei*, see Børresen (1990).

Fathers saw gender as appearing only in the fallen state of 'man'. Gregory Nyssa read the text in this way.[5]

St Augustine also claimed that women possess the image of God in a sex-neutral way, but as female they are not in the image of God. As male to female, it is the male who possesses the image of God, while women are included in it only 'under the male' as their head. Female-ness does not image God but images the bodily creation that the human male is given to rule over.[6] Such an interpretation of the image of God reflects the patriarchal legal and social order in which the paterfamilias or male head of family is the corporate head and representative of the whole *familia*, women, children, slaves, animals and land, under his control. He alone possesses personhood juridically in the public order.

This concept of women as lacking full personhood, as image of God only derivatively, was re-enforced by the scholastic appropriation of Aristotelian biology. This (false) biology asserted that the male alone provides the seed or 'form' of the offspring, while the female contributes only the material substratum that is formed.[7] If this process is fully carried out, and the male seed fully forms the female matter, another male will be born.

Females are the result of a defect in gestation in which the maternal matter fails to be fully formed by the male seed. In this construct of male to female as form to matter (which denies the existence of the female ovum), the female is defined as a defective human, lacking in full humanity, inferior in bodily strength, adequate rationality and moral self-control. These defects preclude both autonomy and rule over others for females, and demand that the woman be subject to the male.

The female, then, is defined by medieval theologians, such as Thomas Aquinas, who appropriates this Aristotelian view, as a non-normative human who lacks the fullness of human nature. The male is the 'perfect' or complete expression of the human species. Aquinas concludes from this anthropology that the maleness of the historical Jesus was an onto-logical necessity, not a historical accident. In order for Jesus as the Christ to represent humanity as a whole, he must be male, because only the male possesses the fullness of human nature. The female cannot represent the human, either for herself or generically.[8]

---

5.   Gregory Nyssa, *De Opif Hom.* 16.7; see Ruether 1974a: 153-55.
6.   Augustine, *De Trinitate* 7.7.10
7.   Aristotle, *Gen. An.* 729b, 737-738.
8.   Thomas Aquinas, *Summa Theologica*, pt.1, q. 92, art. 1.

This interlocking set of ideas about the maleness of God, the Logos of God, the *imago Dei* and Christ threaten to undermine the basic Christian belief that women are included in the redemption of 'man' won by Christ. The Church Fathers assumed she was included, while being humanly non-normative and non-theomorphic, because they assumed a patriarchal ideology in which women are included 'under' a ontological maleness theologically, just as they were included 'under' and represented by the male head of the family juridically, in patriarchal society and law.

Today women have won the rights of citizens or 'civil persons' in the political-juridical order. Higher education, opened to women, has disproved the notion of women's inferior intelligence. Aristotelian biology has been shown to be false. Indeed the actual gestation of the child proceeds in the opposite way, with the female ovum and uterus shaping a female generic fetus, from which a differentiation process must take place in order to make a male.[9] All the androcentric assumptions on which the christological symbols were based have been thrown into question.

Today a Christology that elevates Jesus' human maleness to ontologically necessary significance makes the Christ symbol non-inclusive of women. In order to reaffirm the basic Christian belief that women are included in redemption 'in Christ', all the symbolic underpinnings of Christology must be reinterpreted. Is this possible? What might this mean? In order to reassess the relationship of Christology and gender, we might start by examining the more gender inclusive possibilities of the basic symbols of God and the image of God, Christ and the Logos of God on which Christology was built. We should also ask about Jesus' own teaching and praxis.

Jewish tradition thinks of God as beyond gender. God is thought of as like both a ruler and a parent. This divine ruler-parent sometimes exercises power in wrathful and judgmental ways, but, at other times, can be thought of as merciful, forgiving, compassionate and even as patient and long-suffering. In terms of gender stereotypes, God is androgynous. Sometimes female metaphors are explicitly used for these 'maternal' aspects of God.[10] However, since the male pronoun is used for God, this might suggest that God is an androgynous male.

But Judaism also rejects literalism about verbal or visual images used

9. Sherfey 1972.
10. For example, see Isa. 42.13, 14; 49.14-15. Also Swidler 1979: 21-50.

for God. God is beyond all such creaturely images, and to take any image literally is idolatry. In order to combine these two insights: God's 'androgynous' nature and yet transcendence of all anthropomorphic literalism, we must become clearer about the metaphorical character of such gender images. In God's self, God is neither male or female (or humanly gendered at all). But our metaphors for God must include both male and female. This cannot be done simply by adding together patriarchal masculine and feminine gender stereotypes, or even by giving a male God a 'feminine' side, for this still leaves women without full humanity.

We might use gender symbols in a way that affirms that God both transcends and yet includes the fullness of the humanity of both men and women. Women are rational agents who reflect these qualities of God, while men are affirmed in their caring, nurturing capacities. Only then can we say that both men and women possess the image of God, in mutuality, and yet also as full persons in their own right, and not simply by including women under a male 'head', or as complementary parts of a whole found only as the heterosexual couple.

Another way the Hebrew tradition brought androgyny into God was to picture the immanences of God in female metaphors. The most notable of these is the Wisdom metaphor. Wisdom caring for the cosmos is pictured as like a woman caring for her household.[11] This Wisdom idea is of particular significance for Christians, because, theologically, Wisdom plays the same roles as the Logos (and was the original version of this idea). She is the presence of God as means of creation, revelation and redemption. Jesus' divinity is sometimes identified as the 'Wisdom' of God.[12]

Recognition of the Wisdom version of this concept deliteralizes the metaphor 'Son of God' for the second person of the Trinity. The idea that the immanence of God is like a 'son', or male offspring, in relation to a genitor, or 'father', cannot be taken literally. God as Logos-Sophia is neither male nor female, and can be imaged in both male and female metaphors. We must also ask whether the parent-child metaphor, for imaging the relation of divine transcendence and immanence, needs to be discarded as more misleading than revealing.

But surely, one might say, the Jewish notion of Messiah was always and only a male! The Messiah idea originated as a title for the kings of

11. See Wisdom of Solomon 6–8.
12. Lk. 11.49; Mt. 11.18-19: see Robinson 1975; Schüssler Fiorenza 1975.

Israel and, later, as the ideal and future king of Israel.[13] Although rulers, representing divine sovereignty, were generally thought of as male, female rulers were not unknown in the ancient Middle East. Jesus' own preferred title for the Coming One (who he probably did not identify with himself) was 'ben Adam', usually translated 'Son of Man'. This term, drawn from the book of Daniel and other apocalyptic literature, sees the Messiah as the collective expression of Israel, itself the representative of corporate humanity.

In Jewish liturgy 'ben Adam' refers to females as well as males, despite its androcentric form. Since generic humanity cannot today be seen as normatively male, a more accurate translation of this term would be 'The Human One'. This is the way the *Inclusive Language Lectionary*, prepared by the National Council of Churches of Christ of the USA, chose to translate this term for liturgical reading of Scripture.[14]

From an examination of the symbols used for Christ, we turn to the praxis of the historical Jesus, as interpreted in the Gospels. Here we see the figure of an iconoclastic prophet of God who stands in judgment on social and religious systems that exclude subordinated and marginalized people from divine favor. Jesus' mission is seen as one of bringing 'good news to the poor', hope to despised people whom the priestly and clerical classes regarded as unworthy of redemption. Jesus' prophetic praxis confronts these male leaders for their pretences of special privilege with God and their exclusion of the unlearned and the 'unclean'.

Over against these male leaders, it is often women among the despised groups who are the examples of those who are able to hear God's prophetic word and be converted, while the male elites close their hearts against it. Because women were at the bottom of those systems of privilege decried in the Gospel stories, they become the representatives of the 'last who shall be first in the Kingdom of God'. Luke, in the Magnificat, makes Jesus' mother Mary, potentially despised as one whose child is not her husband's, the exemplar of the messianic community. She is the servant of God who will be lifted up, as the mighty of the world are put down from their thrones.[15]

13. See Mowinckel 1955.

14. See 'Son of Man', in the Inclusive Language Lectionary Committee (1983: appendix).

15. Lk. 1.45-55: See Schaberg (1987: 92-107), for the view that Luke believed Mary's son to be illegitimate, and framed the Magnificat as a statement that God vindicates the most despised of society, the 'fallen' woman.

All four Gospels tell the Jesus story as a drama of mounting conflict in which the messianic prophet is rejected, first by his family and home-town folk, then by the religious leaders, then by the crowd of his popu-lar followers, and then by his own male disciples. It is the core group of his female followers who remain faithful at the cross and are first at the tomb, first witnesses of the resurrection, commissioned by the Risen Lord to take the good news back to the male disciples huddled in the upper room.[16]

Some scholars have rejected this 'empty tomb' story as secondary and unhistorical.[17] But they have failed to ask the question of why all four Gospels tell the story in this way. Is it not to make dramatically clear that despised women, last in the present social and religious order, are the faithful remnant who are first in the redeemed order?

Luke also includes women in his account of Pentecost. Luke uses the text of the prophet Joel to buttress his story of the restoration of the prophetic Spirit to the messianic community, in which the Spirit is given to the 'men servants and the maid servants', and 'your sons and your daughters shall prophesy'.[18] This inclusion of women reflects the fact that women were included in the prophetic office in Hebrew Scrip-ture, as well as in early Christianity.[19] The late second-century church order, the Didache, shows that there were still Christians in that period who saw the prophet as the normative church leader.[20]

Yet the ministry of women was quickly suppressed by an insurgent patriarchal concept of the church.[21] One clue to this repression lies in the ambivalent understanding of the church as messianic community. One group of early Christians understood this apocalyptically, as an impending end of this present world, terminating its mortality and need for reproductive renewal. For them, women have been liberated from traditional gender roles by Christ, since both male and female Christians

---

16. In the synoptic Gospels it is Mary Magdalene who is central to the group of female disciples who are 'last at the cross and first at the tomb'. Although John puts Mary, Jesus' mother, and the disciple John as central figures at the cross, he has the most extended narrative of Mary Magdalene's key role as first witness of the resur-rection. Mary Magdalene plays the key role in gnostic claims for women's apostolic authority: see 'The Gospel of Mary', in Robinson (1977: 471-74).

17. Schillebeeckx 1979: 703 nn. 31-33.

18. Joel 2.28-32; Acts 2.17-21.

19. Schüssler Fiorenza 1979: 39-44.

20. *Didache*, 11.3–13.7.

21. Schüssler Fiorenza 1983.

belonged to a transcendent, heavenly order where marriage and reproduction will be no longer necessary.[22]

The patriarchal churchmen who rejected women's ministry saw the church as part of the existing creational social order. For them the patriarchal, slave-holding social order as still normative for Christian society. The new freedom of women to travel as itinerant preachers, freed by Christ from marriage, was repressed in favor of a Christianity that declared that women were second in Creation, first in sin, are to be silent in church and saved by childbearing.[23]

As we saw in Chapter 2, the conflict between egalitarian, eschatological Christianity and patriarchal historical Christianity continued in the second and third centuries in the gnostic and Montanist struggles.[24] It was resolved in the late fourth–sixth centuries in a new synthesis of the two. In this new synthesis the eschatological ideal of chastity was shorn of its egalitarianism and began to incorporate the patriarchal, clerical leadership class.[25] Marriage, as the life style of most Christians, was reaffirmed, but as a second class, lay stratum of the church.[26]

Celibate women were gradually shorn of the remnants of pastoral ministry and segregated into convents under male episcopal control.[27] The patriarchal, hierarchical church leadership could then be incorporated into the Roman empire as new agents of its rule. This fourth-century synthesis of patriarchal, imperial church organization, together with

22. The alternative Pauline tradition that sees woman as liberated from marriage into itinerant ministry through chastity is expressed in the non-canonical 'Acts of Paul and Thecla'. For interpretations of this conflict between eschatological and patriarchal Paulinisms, see MacDonald (1983).

23. 1 Tim. 2.11-15.

24. Montanist women prophets were accused of abandoning their husbands, which suggests that they shared the view of the Acts of Paul and Thecla that women converts to Christ transcend their marital obligations. Gnostics believed that spiritual rebirth enabled women and men to transcend sex and procreation and enter a state of spiritual androgyny. Both groups supported women in ministry. See Schüssler Fiorenza (1979: 42) and Pagels (1979: 48-69).

25. The Council of Elvira, 400 CE, was the first to mandate clerical continence. The council documents show the connection between clerical sexual continence and obsession with control over female sexuality: see Laeuchli (1972).

26. It became formulaic for fourth-century advocates of asceticism, such as Jerome and Athanasius, to affirm three levels of blessing on female states of life: 100 fold for virginity, 60 fold for continent widowhood and only 30 fold for marriage. See Phipps 1970: 142-75.

27. See Wemple 1983.

a clericalized monastic counter-culture, is passed on as normative Christianity for the next thousand years. Yet a resistance to it from both celibate women and married clerics continued through the Middle Ages.[28]

The Reformation represents a revolt against clerical celibacy. It restored the married clergy, but went on to abolish monasteries for men or women.[29] This meant that it rooted itself all the more exclusively in the patriarchal type of Christianity that saw the patriarchal family as the nucleus of the church, modeled by the married pastor and his obedient wife and children. The household codes become the norm for Christian society with a new force.[30]

But the eschatological counter-culture did not disappear with the suppression of monasticism. Rather it returned in its more radical form, in mystical and millennialist sects, such as the Shakers, who saw the church as a messianic community living in the last days of world history, departing from the evil structures of the worldly society and its church. Freed from gender roles, men and women 'saints' become equal in a new redemptive society. Women again are mandated to preach and prophecy 'in the Spirit', reflecting the new dispensation of the feminine side of God.[31]

We have here two different Christologies and views of the church. Patriarchal Christianity integrates the lordship of Christ with the lordship of Caesar. Christ as divine Logos is the apex of a hierarchical social-political order baptized as Christendom. As delegate of the heavenly Father, Christ rules over the cosmos and is, in turn, the source of the ecclesiastical, political and social hierarchies of church, state and family; clergy over laity, king over subjects and husbands over wives.[32] Women represent the bodily realm that is to be ruled over by the male christological principle in each system of dominance and subjugation.

In the mystical and millennialist Christologies, by contrast, Christ is

28. The period between 500 and 1500 CE saw a continuous struggle of celibate women to retain autonomy and ministry, as well as the resistance of the lower clergy to the imposition of clerical celibacy. See Eckerstein (1898). See Boswell (1980) for the eleventh-century movement to enforce clerical celibacy, seen by the married clergy as a monastic, homosexual movement.

29. There were some notable resistance to Protestant closing of monasteries by nuns. See Douglass 1974.

30. The Puritan leaders place major emphasis on the household for defining marriage: see Perkins (1590) and Gouge (1622).

31. See Irwin 1979: 179-88. Also Ruether 1981.

32. Eusebius, *Oration on Constantine* 10.7.

the transcendent ground of being for the redeemed, who have departed from this fallen world and its corrupt social systems, and are both awaiting and anticipating a redeemed order beyond this world. Christ restores the redeemed to prelapsarian unity and grounds their entrance into heavenly life in Christ by putting aside sexual activity and reproduction. Thereby they recover the sinless and spiritually androgynous mode of being before the fall into sin and death that necessitated gender, sex and reproduction. Since sex, reproduction and family relations are no longer necessary, gender hierarchy can also be abolished. Women, as spiritual peers of men, can participate in equal church leadership.[33]

These two Christologies appear as opposites. But they are both based on a common presupposition, that is, that patriarchy is the order of creation. They assume that patriarchy can only be left behind by leaving the created order. To change this pattern, creation itself must be defined as egalitarian in its original nature. This original egalitarianism must be seen, not as a heavenly state before embodiment, but as our true nature as embodied, historical persons. Only then can patriarchy be placed under judgment as an unjust distortion of our human capacities and social ordering of relationships. Equality between men and women can then be envisioned as a social reform within history that restores our original nature, rather than something possible only by an a-historical departure from history and embodied existence.

As we saw in Chapters 3 and 4, the basis of this egalitarian anthropology was laid in the Society of Friends but only became politically effective by its marriage to political liberalism with its declaration that 'all men are created equal'. Originally this only included white propertied males, leaving intact patriarchal dominance over women, servants and slaves.[34] Gradually it was applied to these subjugated groups; propertyless men, slaves and women.

Today egalitarian anthropology is taken for granted in western society in theory, however much it may be contradicted in practice. Even the Pope and the Catholic bishops now feel compelled to affirm that women are fully human, not inferior or defective in human capacities,

---

33. The nineteenth-century Shakers most fully developed this sexual egalitarianism of the mystical-millennialist tradition. See their bible (Youngs and Green 1856).

34. The reply of John Adams to his wife's exhortation to 'remember the Ladies' in the civil rights of the American Constitution clearly reveals the exclusion, not only of women, but also slaves, Indians and propertyless white servants, from Adams concept of those persons with civil rights: Schneir (1972: 3-4).

and are equal sharers in the 'image of God'. But they cling to a Christology based on a patriarchal anthropology, attempting to use this to exclude women from equality of leadership in the church, while abandoning the more basic exclusion of women from political rights in secular society.[35]

This contradiction between egalitarian anthropology for secular society, and patriarchal Christology for the church hierarchy, reflects a new church–world split. Patriarchy, no longer defensible for secular society, is sacralized as a special sacred order for the church. The result is that Christology loses its basic integration with creation. Christ does not restore and redeem creation, but stands now for a sacred patriarchal order of the church, unconnected with creation. This new creation–redemption split reverses the dilemma of classical Christianity. There creation was assumed to be patriarchal, while redemption in Christ overcame female inferiority, at least spiritually.

In order to recover the integration of Christ and creation essential to a coherent theology, Christology must be recast by integrating it with egalitarian anthropology. Once we have discarded patriarchal anthropology, with its false biological underpinnings, that regarded women as less complete expressions of human nature than men, one must also affirm women as equally theomorphic. If women share equally in the image of God, then they also share equally in the care of creation. This cannot be limited to a dependent, domestic sphere.

If women are equally theomorphic, then God must be imaged as female as well as male, as the ground of that fullness of personhood present in both women and men. This means that the maleness of the historical Jesus has nothing to do with manifesting a divine 'Son' of a divine 'Father'. Both the gender and the parent–child character of these symbols must be deliteralized. God transcendent is the depths of being that we encounter in redemptive experiences, but as one and the same God.

In Jesus we encounter, paradigmatically, the Logos-Sophia of that one God who is both mother and father, liberator, lover and friend. But how do Christians then deal with the maleness of the historical Jesus, if this no longer is seen as ontologically necessary to manifest a male immanence of a male God? Doesn't the very fact that Jesus is a male continue

---

35. This claim to affirm women's secular equality through the concept of *imago Dei* is found in both the pastoral letter on women by John Paul II and the American Catholic bishops pastoral letter on women (see n. 1, above).

the assumption that women receive redemption from men, but cannot represent God as redemptive actors?

Christian feminists cannot resolve this problem by suggesting that, because Jesus was non-patriarchal in his sensitivity to women and in his vulnerability in suffering, that somehow this makes him 'feminine' and thus inclusive of women. All this does is make Jesus a model for an androgynous male, presumably the holistic capacities that every male should develop. But this does nothing to affirm a like holistic humanity for women. Rather, I believe Christians must affirm the particularity of Jesus, not only in gender, but also in ethnicity and culture, and the limitations of any single individual to be universally paradigmatic.

What we find in classical Christology is a dissolution of all other aspects of Jesus' historical particularity, his Jewishness, his first-century cultural setting, while elevating his gender to universal ontological significance. Instead, I believe we should encounter Jesus, not only as male, but in all his particularity as a first-century Galilean Jew. We then must ask how we can see him as paradigmatic of universal human redemption in a way that can apply to female as well as male, to people of all ethnicities and cultures?

This investigation must take us through several stages of revisionist thought about Christology. First, we must see that what is paradigmatic about Jesus is not his biological ontology, but rather his person as lived message and practice. Jesus becomes paradigmatic by embodying a certain message. That message is good news to the poor, the confrontation with systems of religion and society that incarnate oppressive privilege, and affirmation of the despised as loved and liberated by God. Jesus did not just speak this message; he risked his life to embody this presence of God and was crucified by those in power who rejected this message.

Secondly, we must cease to isolate the work of Christ from the ongoing Christian community. This Jesus we find as a historical figure exemplifies a way of life that is still critical, in a world where false and oppressive privilege still reign, which are still sacralized by religion. As Christians we are followers of this way. While Jesus is the foundational representative of this way of the cross and liberation, he is not its exclusive possibility. Each Christian must also take up this same way and, in so doing, become 'other Christs' to one another. The church becomes redemptive community, not by passively receiving a redemption 'won' by Christ alone, but rather by collectively embodying this path of liberation in a way that transforms people and social systems.

If we are clear that the redemption signified by Christ is both carried on and communicated through redemptive community, this means that Christ can take on the face of every person and group and their diverse liberation struggles. We must be able to encounter Christ as black, as Asian, as Aboriginal, as woman. This also means that the coming Christ, the incompleted future of redemption, is not the historical Jesus returned, but rather the fullness of all this human diversity gathered together in redemptive community. This is the 'Human One' who is to come, who bears the face of all suffering creatures longing for liberation.

Finally, this way of Christ need not and should not be seen as excluding other ways. The creating, inspiriting and liberating presence of God is present to all humans in all times and places. It has been expressed in many religious cultures, some of which parallel the Christ way, and some of which complement it with other spiritualities, spiritualities of contemplation, for example, or of renewal of nature. The challenge of Christology today may be not to try to extend the Christ symbol to every possible spirituality and culture, but rather to accept its limits. Then we can allow other ways and peoples to flourish in dialogues that can reveal God's many words to us.

Chapter Seven

Suffering and Redemption: The Cross and Atonement in Feminist Theology

Suffering challenges the human understanding of reality. The tendency of many cultures is to look for someone or something to blame. To think that suffering is random and meaningless is frightening. By finding a 'cause' one gives meaning to suffering. Human cultures have come up with various 'causes' of suffering. One explanation found in African cultures, among others, is to assume that evil spirits cause illnesses, accidents and misfortunes. Particular people in the village are designated as the agents of these evil spirits and are isolated or punished accordingly.

Women are the favored victims of this explanation for suffering, including accidents that befall their husband and children. Even a woman who miscarries is presumed to have done something amiss to have caused this misfortune and is pressured to confess even on her recovery bed.[1] In Western Europe in the late medieval and Reformation eras this folk tradition of woman-blaming for misfortunes, as the likely vehicles of demonic spirits, was transformed into a campaign of witch persecution by both Catholics and Protestants. Christian teachers used the idea that women are innately weaker and prone to evil, having caused evil to enter the world in the first place, to scapegoat women as witches, often those that were poor, marginal or nonconformist.[2]

---

1. See, for example, Oduyoye 1992: 14; also Oduyoye 1995: 40-42, 120-23; and Amoah 1990: 129-53.
2. Catholic theological misogyny as a rationale for why most witches are female is found in the fifteenth century Dominican handbook for witch-hunting, *Malleus Maleficarum* (trans. Montague Summers; New York: Dover, 1971). The sixteenth-century Calvinist theologian William Perkins gave a similar if less extensive rationale from a Reform perspective: see his 'The Damned Art of Witchcraft', in Perkins (1970: 596). For a discussion of the relation of women, religion and witchcraft

The classic explanation for misfortunes developed in ancient Judaism was that it was caused by human sin. This was particularly applied to collective misfortunes that befell the nation. Both natural disasters, such as droughts and floods, and also devastating incursions by foreign armies that trampled over fields, looted and killed and carried the survivors into exile, were explained as divine punishment by Israel's God. Israel has failed to obey God's commandments and so has suffered. The experiences of disasters thus became the occasion for prophets and teachers to call for repentance, return to strict observance of God's commandments, in order to restore God's favor, Israel's return to its promised land and a time of peace and prosperity.[3]

The writer of the book of Job challenged this explanation for suffering, insisting on the innocence of the righteous Job, who had done nothing to deserve such suffering. The answer God gives Job from the whirlwind does not give an alternative explanation, but simply an awesome demonstration of God's sovereign power over all that transpires in creation, before whose might puny humans should fall silent.[4] 'Who are you to question God's ways?' is God's answer to the problem of suffering, but an answer which begs the question.

The question of innocent suffering, particularly innocent suffering of the nation as a whole, has plagued Jewish thought through the centuries, as its people have been victimized by successive powerful empires. This question has returned with new urgency after the Nazi Holocaust, causing thoughtful Jewish thinkers to question the very idea of a just God who is in charge of history.[5] The dilemma of theodicy: that God is either unable to stop suffering and hence not omnipotent, or else wills unjust suffering and hence not good, haunts post-Holocaust Jewish thought.

For Christians, however, the question of the Holocaust is not directed at God's goodness or power, but at their own complicity. Since the

persecution, see Ruether 1995b: 89-114. Also the chapter on witchcraft in Weisner 1993: 218-38.

3.   This announcement that divine punishment is about to befall Israel due to its sin and disobedience is typical of the prophetic writings; see for example the book of Amos.

4.   Job 38.1–40.2.

5.   The major Jewish Holocaust theologians are Richard Rubenstein, Emil Fackenheim and Irving Greenberg: see Ruether and Ruether (1989: 191-203); for a Jewish critique of the abuse of Holocaust theology to justify injustice to Palestinians by the state of Israel, see Ellis (1990, 1994).

Holocaust in Nazi Germany drew on a heritage of more than a millennium of Christian religious hatred and persecution of Jews, Christians must ask themselves what in their own teaching fueled such hatred and how are these Christian teachings on Jews and Judaism to be changed to purge them of anti-Semitism.[6]

Traditionally the Christian response to suffering has been a complex synthesis of human self-blaming and a view of God who is both omnipotent and yet a compassionate savior who intervenes in history, sending his 'own son' to suffer and die to rescue humans from their sinful condition. Both God's power and goodness are vindicated in the face of suffering by teaching that God voluntarily takes on human suffering and pays for the primal sin that is its cause. This combination of beliefs makes for a powerful construction both to answer the question of suffering and silence the question, but when the threads of its fabric are examined, it threatens to unravel.

The Christian answer combines the following set of claims. First, it is said that God created a wholly good creation and intended the human condition to be painless. There was neither moral nor physical evil in God's original plan. Originally humans would neither have sinned nor died. Human disobedience, initiated by women, who bear the primary guilt for it, ruined this original plan and corrupted human nature and the natural world itself. As a result humans sank into a condition where they are both prone to physical evils, culminating in death, and are locked in a tendency to moral evil from which they are unable to rescue themselves, having lost their original free will. God is saved from any responsibility for evil, moral or 'natural', which is placed totally on human, especially female, shoulders.

Secondly, humans are said to have incurred an infinite guilt for this situation of evil that they are incapable of paying. They have offended God infinitely and are thereby irreparably alienated from God, without any means at their disposal to make amends. But God in his graciousness has intervened to overcome this alienation and pay for this guilt. This gulf between humans and God can only be bridged through a blood sacrifice of one who is both 'man', but one innocent of sin, and God. Through voluntarily suffering and dying on the cross as one himself lacking in sin and hence guilt for it, Jesus pays for human sin as a human

---

6. For Christian Holocaust theology, see Ruether and Ruether (1989: 203-15); also Ruether (1974b).

and also acts as God to bridge the gulf created by human guilt that only God, not humans, can overcome.

The good news of redemption through the cross is that we are reconciled with God, and God now loves and accepts us in spite of our sin. We now have the possibility of growing in moral goodness through divine grace, gifted by a new capacity to obey God that we are incapable of in our present human condition, but receive through a power that comes to us from God. By accepting this good news that we are accepted, even while still sinners (and continuing to be sinners), we are assured of ultimately overcoming the mortality into which we were plunged through sin and living happily with God after death.

But what of continuing suffering here and now on earth? What of injustices that bring terrible suffering to the innocent; what about natural disasters that destroy human efforts to build secure lives? Although some Christians have held out the hope that either apocalyptic intervention from God or human progress would bring about a new paradise on earth,[7] mainline Christianity has offered no promise that anything will get better on earth, either morally or physically, as a result of the redemption won by the cross of Christ. The action of the god-man is vertical, changing alienation from God to acceptance by God, not horizontal, changing evils that plague human history.

Sufferings, both those caused by unjust evils and by inexplicable 'natural' disasters and mortality, continue unchanged by the cross of Christ. The Christian response to this continued reign of suffering on earth is a peculiar double bind. On the one hand, one should regard oneself as guilty for such continued suffering, and redouble one's repentance for guilt, and gratitude to Christ for having overcome a guilt we cannot overcome by ourselves. Indeed all other sufferings are said to pale before the sufferings endured by Christ on the cross for our sins, and it is we who caused Christ to suffer. If we had not caused sin in the first place, Christ would not have had to suffer to rescue us. Our contemplation of Christ's cross therefore should mingle gratitude for overcoming our offense with renewed guilt at having caused the terrible offense that made this infinite suffering necessary.

Secondly, even if we are innocent of having caused some particular evil that befalls us, we should endure it, accepting its blows, because thereby we imitate the cross of Christ. We become Christlike by enduring suffering like Christ, who, though innocent, suffered for our sins.

---

7.   For Christian traditions of future hope, see Chapter 8 below.

Significantly this double-bind message of the cross is first developed in the New Testament as a way of counselling slaves to passively accept not only the condition of slavery itself, but also the arbitrary beatings often inflicted on them by their masters.

> Slaves, accept the authority of your masters with all deference, not only those who are kind and gentle, but also those who are harsh. For it is a credit to you if, being aware of God, you endure pain while suffering unjustly. If you endure when you are beaten for doing wrong, what credit is that? But if you endure when you do right and suffer for it, you have God's approval. For to this you have been called, because Christ also suffered for you, leaving you an example, so that you could follow in his steps.[8]

From medieval times to the present this double-bind message of the cross has been particularly preached to Christian women to accept not only their condition of subjugation, but also arbitrary violence visited upon them by husbands.[9] On the one hand, women are doubly guilty for the primal guilt of humanity (if it is possible to be doubly guilty of an infinite guilt). In any case women were created to be subjected to men in God's original plan for creation, but their disobedience caused them to be punished by a redoubled servitude justly enforced coercively. So women should regard the general conditions of their harsh subjugation as both their 'natural' condition and as just punishment for their sin.

Women should endure even harsh enforcement of their subjugation as their due both by nature and a punishment for their sin. But if in some particular situation this harshness becomes excessive, and they are blameless of any particular offense that might have occasioned it, then this too they should endure without complaint, since by sweetly accepting unjust suffering they become Christlike. The hope is held out that their cruel husbands may eventually be converted by this sweet acceptance of cruelty, reminded of Christ's suffering for them.[10] Thus the

---

8. 1 Pet. 2.18-21 (NRSV).

9. In Chaucer's *The Canterbury Tales*, the story of the patient Griselda who endures without complaint the extreme suffering and arbitrary trials imposed on her by her husband is told as a model of wifely decorum; see 'The Clerk's Tale', in Chaucer (1932: 197-218).

10. For a critique of the way the cross is used to perpetuate wife battering, see the DMin thesis by Carole Findon (1995).

cross of Christ has become an exquisite tool for justifying domestic violence and advising women to endure it without complaint.

This double bind of deserved suffering for guilt and the promise of becoming a Christlike agent of redemption for one's victimizers through innocent suffering has been such a powerful message that Christian women have found it very difficult to challenge. Even feminist theology has only gradually linked the Eve myth with the theology of the cross. Feminist theology early began to unpack the myth of Eve, with its views of female innate subordination and guilt for evil. But they have been slow to question the theology of Christ's sufferings as a model for women's sufferings. Dare we ask: are we saved by the innocent suffering of Christ on the cross? This means asking, not only is Christ's innocent suffering on the cross a model of us, but is it redemptive in itself?

Joanne Carlson Brown and Rebecca Parker's article 'For God so Loved the World' was the major piece that opened up this question of redemptive suffering.[11] In this article Brown and Parker critique the 'satisfaction' theory of atonement through the blood of Christ on the cross. They show how this theory of atonement reproduces a sado-masochistic theology and practice based on the idea of an 'offended' God who can only be mollified through the payment of innocent blood by one who is both human and divine. This theology has been used to make women both the guilty ones deserving of suffering and the suffering servants called to imitate the innocent Christ.

Brown and Parker also question the 'moral influence' theory of atonement, shaped by Abelard in the twelfth century as an alternative to Anselm's 'satisfaction' theory. Abelard questioned the view of God as one whose anger needs to be assuaged through the blood of an innocent victim. In his view it is our, not God's, attitudes that need to be changed. God continues to love us and to want our repentance, but our hearts are hardened through sin. By seeing the proof of God's love for us even unto death through the suffering victim, Christ, we are converted.[12]

Brown and Parker also question Abelard's theory as one that condones suffering and death. A version of this theory has also been proposed to women who, through patient suffering at the hands of battering husbands, are supposed to change their hearts. Likewise modern spiritualities of non-violent struggle, as proposed by martyrs, such as

---

11. In Brown and Bohn 1980: 1-30.
12. Brown and Bohn 1980a: 11-13.

Martin Luther King, Gandhi and Archbishop Romero, have counselled those who want to transform the hard hearts of their oppressors to endure unjust suffering.

It may be right to struggle without recourse to violence for other reasons. But there is little evidence that oppressors' hearts are changed by seeing the sufferings of their victims. Rather they intend this suffering and death in order to silence those they wish to eliminate. Their own followers may be inspired by the memory of their leaders' unjust torture and death to continue the struggle, but is this a reason to propose an embrace of torture and assassination?

For Brown and Parker a feminist liberation theology of redemption must start with the proposition that unjust suffering and death are never justified as a means of redemption. We are not redeemed through or because of anyone's unjust torture and death, including that of Jesus. Rather redemption means a transformation that brings abundant life in loving mutuality. Redemption comes about through processes or practices that actually create and promote mutual flourishing.

Unjust suffering and death is the opposite of redemption and does not substantially promote it. Prophetic figures who confront oppressive powers and call for a transformation of hearts and social systems toward just and loving life are killed by those who benefit from unjust power in order to stop them from promoting such alternatives. They wish to silence them and to terrorize their followers into silence. The desired effect of the public torture of prophets to death is to scatter their followers in dismay.

This is exactly what happened with Jesus' followers, but they then became convinced that he was not dead but risen, and they reassembled to continue his proclamation of 'good news'. This did not come about through or because of the cross, but as a refusal to accept the message of the cross, an insistence that life will win over death in the end. For Brown and Parker we need to distinguish Jesus' proclamation of justice and abundance of life in the face of oppressors, and his disciples' renewed courage to continue his proclamation, from the cross as a crime intended to silence him and to destroy his movement.

Womanist theologian Delores Williams has made a similar critique of the doctrine of atonement through the blood of the cross. For Williams, the figure of the Egyptian slave woman, Hagar, who was forced to become a surrogate mother to bear a child for her childless master and mistress, Sarai and Abraham, and then cast into the wilderness, only to find there an encounter with God and hope for the future, is a paradigm of African-American women's experiences. Like Hagar, African-American women in slavery times were made surrogate sex objects and child-bearers, as well as oppressed workers, for their masters. They fled into the wilderness to find freedom.[13]

For Williams, redemption must be judged in terms of black women's oppression and their struggle for survival and 'quality of life' for them-selves and their children. Black women encounter a redeeming God, not through Christ's sufferings on the cross, but in wilderness experi-ences where they encounter a God that gives them the power and hope to 'find a way where there is no way'. For Williams, the theology of atonement that makes the innocent sufferings of Jesus on the cross a surrogate for sinful humanity re-enforces unjust suffering, particularly the surrogate suffering that black women have had to endure. The cross needs to be recognized as a symbol of evil, not a means of redemption. It expresses the efforts of those who rejected Jesus' ministry to destroy his movement by killing him.

The cross can be seen as an extreme example of the risk that anyone struggling against oppression takes at the hands of those who want to keep the systems of domination intact, but it is not itself redeeming. What is redeeming is not Jesus' sufferings and death, but his life, his vision of justice and right relation restored in communities of celebra-tion and abundant life. Jesus is a model and helper for black women as one who resisted the temptations toward unjust power in the wilderness and spoke the word of life against the systems of death. It is this ministry of healing and prophetic proclamation on behalf of life that black women need to imitate as followers of Jesus. Although we may fall prey to the powers of oppression in so doing, this is not to be sought, nor is it a way of promoting redemptive life.[14]

European feminist theologian Dorothee Soelle has also struggled with the theology of atonement through the cross, but from a different per-spective from Brown and Parker and Delores Williams. Soelle focuses on the problem of rich complacent white Christians who benefit from the violence of an oppressive world. Soelle sees the traditional Christian message that we are powerless sinners who can only passively receive our redemption from above as re-enforcing a spirituality and ethic of passive collaboration with the powers of violence and oppression. We

13. Williams 1993b.
14. Williams 1991: 1-14.

need to break through this collaboration by rejecting the notion of a patriarchal God who created systems of domination and who calls us to obedient service to them.

Jesus reveals the true God as one who unmasks the systems of evil and shows them to be demonic. Jesus announces the true God who is on the side of the poor and the victimized of oppressive society. In so doing he runs the risk of retaliation by those in power. The cross is the ultimate expression of this retaliation by the mighty of religion and state that rejected his call for repentance and solidarity with the poor and sought to shore up their own system of power and its ideological justifications by silencing the prophet.

The resurrection means that they did not succeed in silencing him. He rose and continues to rise wherever prophets arise, breaking through the system of lies, and offering a glimpse of the true God of life who stands against the evil systems of worldly power. The cross is not a payment for sin, or a required sacrifice for our well-being, but the risk that Jesus and all people take whem they unmask the idols and announce the good news that God is on the side of the poor and those who struggle for justice.[15]

For Soelle the resurrection is a victory over the cross, but this does not mean that the cross itself was necessary nor is it in itself redemptive. Rather redemption happens whenever we resist and reject collaboration with injustice and begin to taste the joys of true well-being in mutual service and shared life. When life is lived in solidarity with others in mutual well-being, every act of sustaining life becomes a sacrament of God's presence, whether this is bread broken and shared, sexual pleasure between lovers, tilling the ground, making a useful product or giving birth to a baby. God calls us into abundance of life here on earth. This is the promise of God's Kingdom when 'God's will is done on earth, as it is in heaven.'[16]

Another aspect of this critique of the traditional theology of sin and atonement through the cross has come from Korean Minjung theology. For Minjung theologians, such as Andrew Park and Chung Hyun Kyung, Christian theology has focused too much on the idea of sin as pride and not enough on the experiences of oppression by those victimized by the pride of others. Sin as prideful disobedience to God and violence to others is the evil done by those in power. It is important to

15. Soelle 1995a: 99-108.
16. Soelle 1995b: 41-48; Soelle 1990: 12-22.

critique this kind of sinful evil, but it should not be universalized as the situation of all humans. Rather the majority of humans have been shaped, not by overweening pride in dominating power, but by the sorrows and sufferings of victimized suffering. This is what Minjung theology calls 'Han'.[17]

Han is the frustrated sorrow and anger at unjust suffering accumulated in the masses of people (the Minjung) due to the repression of any outlet for this anger or resolution to their experiences of injustice. Han is not simply an experience of individuals, but it is collective and transmitted from generation to generation. It can find dangerous expression in explosions of mass anger. It can also find creative expression in the masked dances and folk dramas of Korean villagers, who thereby mock the authorities and demystify their claims of obedient respect. Han also is the tenacity for life that continually arises in the people in the midst of situations of crushing defeat.

Minjung theologians recognize Han in the individual and collective expression of the people's sorrow and anger, but also in their resistance to unjust suffering. They seek to convert this resistance into constructive power to protest injustice and to engage in struggle to change it.[18] From this Minjung perspective, the cross of Jesus is an expression of sin, that is, the evil of the dominant powers who seek to perpetuate their power by silencing the one who calls for conversion.

But the cross does not atone for sin. Rather those who remember the cross as a crime against humanity experience the Han of accumulated anger and sorrow at this act of unjust violence, but they also revolt against it by carrying on Jesus' message of good news to the poor.[19] The resurrection manifests the tenacity for life that rises in the victimized who refuse to accept the power of the rulers to silence the prophets. Redemption takes place in the continual resurgence of power and hope for abundant life that sustains the struggle against the system of death.

These feminist liberation critiques of the classical theology of the cross should force Christian theologians and liturgists to tell the Jesus story in a different way, a way that I believe is more authentic to its historical reality. Jesus did not 'come to suffer and die'. Rather Jesus conceived of his mission as one of 'good news to the poor, the liberation of the cap-

---

17. Park 1993.

18. Kyung 1990b: 134-46.

19. This is my own application of the theology of Han to the cross, not one developed explicitly by Park or Chung.

tive', that is, experiences of liberation and abundance of life shared between those who had been on the underside of the dominant systems of religion and state of his time.

Jesus shared these experiences of liberating life for the poor and revealed a liberating God by exorcisms and healings and by celebratory meals in which marginalized people shared food at table together. He did not seek to be killed by the powers that be, but rather to convert them into solidarity with those they had formerly despised and victimized. He offered to them also an entry into the Kingdom of God, but only by following after 'the prostitute and the tax collectors', that is, those they formerly regarded as unclean and unworthy.[20]

The poor heard him gladly, but those in power refused his invitation of conversion. They sought to silence him and destroy his community of followers by subjecting him to a terrorizing public execution. The notions that he 'willingly' accepted this death, and even that he sought it as the necessary means of redemption, are later Christian rationalizations in the face of the terrible reality of the crucifixion. This is belied by the cry of Jesus from the cross, 'My God, my God, why has thou forsaken me', suggesting one who hoped that God would bring about transforming new life, not the handing him over to the power of the oppressors.[21]

Like other prophets who see that the power of those who want to silence them is mounting, he may have recognized shortly before his death that it was likely that they would 'get him'. But this is quite different from conceiving of crucifixion as something to be sought and accepted as a means of redemption. Rather we should say that redemption happens through resistance to the sway of evil, and in the experiences of conversion and healing by which communities of well-being are created. Jesus practiced such healing and community gathering and called for the conversion of the dominant into repentant solidarity. We follow him by continuing this same struggle for life against unjust suffering and death.

If Jesus came to give us a glimpse of abundant life liberated from the oppressive powers and the prophetic courage to confront and call for

---

20. Mt. 21.31. Matthew uses this saying of Jesus to suggest that the Pharisees are unbelievers who will never be converted and go into the Kingdom; but the saying suggests an earlier context in which the Pharisees are called to be converted, but the condition of their conversion is a solidarity with those they despise in which they go into the Kingdom of God 'behind' them (my own interpretation).

21. Mk 15.34; also Mt. 27.46.

the conversion of those who profit from unjust power, what of the finitude of life itself? Will not these tastes of abundant life themselves pass away in death as the fragility of finite life catches up even with communities of joyful celebration? In the history of the interpretation of the cross we see a prophetic spirituality that sought to confront one problem, namely unjust suffering caused by sinful human systems, pressed into the service of solving another problem, namely, mortality. This was not Jesus' issue, but the issue of Greek spirituality. The Greeks were concerned with death as a problem of finitude, rather than unjust death visited upon the advocates of the poor by the powerful.

We should not call people who experience life's tragic vicissitudes to 'carry their cross'. Even in the face of 'natural' ills, we should not passively acquiesce (itself a sure means of hastening death), but cultivate the resiliency of life that allows us to live abundantly even in the midst of the fragilities and limits of life. The contemplative spiritualities of the world's religious traditions have been about cultivating this spirit of resiliency in the midst of finitude, letting go of ego-clinging and cultivating compassion for all 'sentient beings', to use Buddhist language.

Perhaps we need a complementarity of spiritualities appropriate in different situations. There is a place for the contemplative spirituality that learns to be in communion with God in the midst of finitude, and there is a time for the prophetic spirituality that gives us the courage to resist unjust evils, call for the overthrow of oppression, the conversion of oppressors and the gathering of counter-cultural communities of life. We need to cultivate both but not confuse these two spiritualites, just as we should not confuse the death from unjust violence we need to protest with the finitude that will bring natural death at the end, hopefully, of a full life.

Where is God in all this? If Jesus unmasks the God who justifies systems of violence, and reveals the true God on the side of the poor, what God reigns in the crucifixion of Jesus and in continued unjust suffering and the killing of the prophets? The God of omnipotent control over history and the God of good news to the poor are incompatible. If God wills Jesus' death, if God wills the unjust violence of poverty, sexism, racism and anti-Semitism, then God is a sadist and a criminal.

The God who is on the side of the poor is not in power in the history in which crime continues to win. Divine goodness and divine omnipotence cannot be reconciled, as Christianity has sought to do in the theology of atonement. Rather, in so far as God represents just and loving life in mutual sharing, God is for us the insurgent tenacity of life that is not in the seats of power, but yet is still undefeated.

This good and holy power for life continually arises, despite the victories of unjust death, to empower new struggles for well-being, sustaining the moment glimpses where this well-being is lived here and now. The God of the resurrection did not cause the cross, but was momentarily crushed by the cross, only to rise again, overcoming it with a rebirth of protest and new hope. In the resurrection we say No to unjust death and Yes to life abundant for all of us together.

Chapter Eight

Future Hope and Eschatology
in Feminist Theology

As we have seen in Chapter 1 of this study, the original meaning of the word 'redemption' in Hebrew Scripture referred neither to life after death nor to a comprehensive millennial hope, but to the very concrete act of 'redeeming' or ransoming a slave from servitude. From this root meaning, it acquired a collective national meaning referring to God's past act of rescuing Israel from slavery in Egypt. As the idea of a future national hope emerged, it grounded itself on this foundational past act of God. Israel looked forward to a future in which it would be definitively rescued from bondage to surrounding imperial powers.

This future hope took on cosmological dimensions: hope for the release of all humanity from injustice and the blossoming of paradisaical conditions on earth. But the root meaning of redemption remained historical and this-worldly; a release from body and soul-crushing servitude into freedom and flourishing life. But none of these ideas assumed an escape from the basic conditions of mortality. Hebrew thought for most of the biblical period assumed that mortality was the 'natural' human condition, and shaped its hope for the 'good life' within those limits, not escape from them.

A second tradition developed in Babylonian and Egyptian religions and was transformed in Greek philosophical thought. It saw mortality itself as the problem. It imagined the soul as preexisting the body in some heavenly realm, descending to earth, taking on mortal components and then escaping it at death. The mortal body was seen as alien to the immortal nature of the soul. Rites and practices of purification aimed to free the soul from the body so it could return to its heavenly home in the stars.[1]

1. Cumont 1912: Ch. 6.

A third tradition that emerged in Persian religion imagined world history as a conflict between good and evil world powers. The history of the world was divided into four periods, each three thousand years long, reflecting successive stages in the conflict of these two cosmic powers for possession of the earth. In the first period the two powers remain apart, each producing their own spiritual creatures. In the second period the material creation appears and the two powers war over it. In the third period the evil power establishes his ascendancy over the earth.

The final era begins with the birth of Zoroaster and the spread of true religion, from which will flow a gradual victory of good over evil. Three good rulers or Saoshayants (saviors) reign over each successive thousand-year period, in which both moral and physical evils are gradually overcome. Then the final savior appears and inaugurates the 'last things'. He raises the dead, beginning with Gayomard (the first or primal man). All humanity, past and present, will assemble and be judged for their good and bad deeds. The righteous and the wicked are separated. The wicked are punished for three days in hell and weep for their sins, while the righteous in heaven weep for them. This period of repentance and mourning is followed by cosmic transformation. The mountains are melted down into a molten river, and all humans pass through it and are purged from the tendency to evil. The Savior then sacrifices the cosmic beast and prepares a feast for all humans, making them immortal. The evil spirit is destroyed, Hell itself purified and reclaimed 'for the enlargement of the world', and all live together forever on an earth made blessed and everlasting.[2]

This Persian vision of world history would have a profound effect on Jewish and Christian thought, shaping future historical hope into apocalyptic narratives in the era between the Testaments. Millennialist and apocalyptic thought continues to be revived in Christianity in new versions, reflecting new calculations of contemporary world crises, up to the present time.[3] The legacy of Christian thought in regard to the meaning of redemption thus continues to today to mingle, in complex and often contradictory ways, these three traditions: prophetic historical hope, cosmological apocalyptic and personal immortality of the soul freed from the body to ascend to a spiritual realm after death.

2.   *The Bundahis*, in West (1965: V, 1-151).
3.   Ruether 1992: 61-84.

Historical Development

In this section of the chapter, I will flesh out in some more detail the history of the development and intertwining of these traditions. I will then reflect on the problems with each tradition from the perspective of their views of gender. To what extent have each of these views advanced or negated women's hope for delivery from sexism? How does feminist theology address questions of historical hope, or the overcoming of patriarchal injustices, on the one hand, and the quest to escape from death, on the other? I will also ask about the ecological dimensions of these views? Has the quest to escape from the body and the earth fueled a contempt for nature, as well as for women?

The ancient civilizations of the Near East, the Sumerians and the Babylonians, did not hold out any hope for personal immortality. They saw death as that which separated mortals from immortals, that is, humans from gods. The great Babylonian epic *Gilgamesh* has as its main theme the futility of man's quest for immortality. Gilgamesh discovers the plant of immortality, but its possession eludes his grasp. In the course of his journey, an alewife, representing perhaps female folk wisdom, counsels him to give up this useless search and to enjoy the good things of mortal life:

> Gilgamesh, whither rovest thou?
> The life thou pursuest thou shall not find.
> When the gods created humans,
> death for humankind they set aside;
> Life in their own hands retaining.[4]

The primary focus of Sumerian and Babylonian religions was on seasonal renewal. By ritual participation in the yearly liturgies by which the powers of drought and death in nature are defeated and the new rains bring the rise of new life in the seasonal planting and harvest, they hoped to assure the miracle of new birth for plants, animals and humans on which their lives depended. This life cycle in nature was represented by stories of the defeat and dismembering of a God, representing the vegetation, by an enemy 'brother' who represented drought and death.

Through the mediation of a goddess sister-spouse, the body of the dead God was reassembled and planted, bringing about the rise of the new powers of life wedded anew to his goddess wife, through whom

---

4. *The Epic of Gilgamesh*, Tablet X.3, in Mendelson (1955: 92).

the powers of birth are renewed.[5] This seasonal 'resurrection from the dead' into new life has been the realistic focus of the hopes of indigenous religions around the world. We will return to this understanding of future hope as seasonal renewal within the life cycle in our discussion of ecology.

Hebrew prophetic thought broke with this religion of the seasonal life cycle for a new emphasis on social justice. The nature religions of the Near Eastern world accepted not only mortality, but the social hierarchy of master and slave as the unchangeable condition decreed by the gods. Humans themselves were said to have been created to be the 'slaves of the gods' so the gods could be at leisure.[6] Thus the god–human relation was interpreted in a way that re-enforced the gulf, not only between mortals and immortals, but between masters and slaves.

By contrast, Hebrew prophetic thought came to formulate the condition of slavery as unjust and to shape their understanding of their special relation to God as one who delivers slaves from servitude. They thus shaped an understanding of religion that challenges the social hierarchies of rich over poor, master over slaves, and the great empires over the weak, easily conquered peoples. The vision of God as redeemer who saved them from slavery in Egypt was extended to a hope for deliverance of history itself from the conditions of injustice, bringing about a new age in which all life on earth would flourish in harmonious abundance.

By contrast, their Egyptian imperial neighbors focused on an escape from death that at first was limited to royalty and only later applied to wealthy lesser mortals, although never including slaves, except as those who might go with their embalmed masters into an eternal servitude. Happy immortal life was a class privilege. Through the expensive rites of embalming and secure entombment in stone chambers, they hoped to preserve the essential self from its corruption of the body.[7]

In Babylonian culture the cultivation of astronomy led to speculation on the stars as the dwelling place of the gods and of human souls as lesser sparks of divine life. They imaged a 'soul journey' in which the soul descends from its heavenly home, absorbs the influence of each

---

5. For example the Poems of Anath and Baal reflect this mythic story: see Mendelson (1995: 224-61).

6. See the Babylonian creation epic, the Enuma Elish (Mendelson 1995: 17-46).

7. See Wallis Budge 1961.

planet as its passes through the seven planetary levels, to take on the fleshy body on earth. Special rites, amulets and prayers could facilitate the return journey of the soul, in which it doffs the body and the planetary influences that tie it to mortal and sensual life and reclaims its original pure and immortal existence in its 'native star'.[8]

This Babylonian soul journey was taken over by Plato and became the core of his understanding of the original and future life of the soul in his creation story, the *Timaeus*, as well as such writings as the *Phaedrus*, where he charts the story of the soul's fall into the body and its stages of escape from the body. In the first two centuries of the Christian era this Babylonian–Platonic myth of the soul's descent and ascent became the focus of mystical salvation religions that promised the soul's escape from the body and the earth into immortal life in the heavens for those who underwent their rites of initiation and lived according to their rules of physical and moral purification.[9]

For the Jewish people living at the crossroads of successive empires of antiquity, Egyptian, Assyrian, Persian, Greek and Roman, the modest hopes for a flourishing independent national life grew increasingly difficult to imagine, as their people were overrun, reduced to servitude and transported into exile by successive conquerors. Taking over the Persian story of world history as cosmic conflict and deliverance from evil, they reshaped this into apocalyptic narratives that were both more nationalistic and more vengeful than that found in Zoroastrian tradition.

They imagined God and his angels defeating the evil powers represented by their enemies and casting them into an eternal perdition. Christianity would add to this more particularist and vengeful version of apocalyptic. In the book of Revelations that concludes the New Testament, Satan and his evil hosts lie behind the evil Roman empire. The saints are Christian believers. God will hurl not only Satan and his devils, but his human minions into eternal fire, while the saints rejoice at the sight. God then creates a new heaven and earth in which both physical and moral evil are banished and death is no more, but this immortal paradise is reserved for the elect few.[10]

However, Judaism at the time of the rise of Christianity also produced other lines of thought. More traditional Sadducees rejected the new

8.   See Chapter 8 n. 1.

9.   This pattern is exhibited in the Hermetic text, *The Poimandres of Hermes Trismegistus*: see Jonas (1963: 152-53).

10.   The book of Revelations 17–22.

apocalyptic theories with their expectation of a future resurrection and judgment of the dead.[11] Philosophically-minded Jews in the Greek city of Alexandria, such as Philo, produced an amalgamation of Jewish ritual and ethics with Platonic mysticism. Through mystical contemplation and bodily disciplines, including celibacy, Philo hoped to liberate the soul from the body and assure its heavenly bliss.[12]

Early Christianity, far from having a uniform eschatology, represents eclectic mixtures of these various traditions in its first three centuries. The Jesus movement seems to have focused more on a this-worldly hope for a reign of God on earth in which the disparities of gender, ethnicity and servitude would be overcome in a new inclusive community of harmony and peace. But other Christians embraced the visions of apocalyptic vengeance against the empire, while yet others were attracted to mystical visions of the deliverance from moral and physical corruption into a immortal life.

As we have seen in Chapter 1, early Christians were divided on whether this transformation takes place radically in baptism and can be lived here and now, or whether it is mostly future. Complex thinkers, such as Paul and the author of the Gospel of John, made distinct and daring syntheses of these traditions of personal, social and cosmological transformation.

As Christianity developed toward the form that became the established Catholic Church of the fourth century, apocalyptic visions of divine vengeance were banished, and the emphasis fell rather on a view of salvation through Christ that assured the soul of immortal life, aided for a spiritual élite by practices of ascetic and contemplative life. Yet apocalyptic visions, not only of divine wrath poured out on the powerful of the earth, but also a future transformation of the earth that would liberate the oppressed, continued to flourish on the underside of Christianity.

Apocalyptic forms of Christianity would rise again and again in protest movements, from the North African Donatists that battled Augustine in the fourth and fifth centuries, to the medieval Waldensians, spiritual Franciscans and Hussites, to the radical movements on the left wing of the sixteenth–seventeenth-century Reformation, such as Diggers,

11. 'They [the Sadducees] accepted only the written Torah and rejected oral law, the doctrine of resurrection and the current belief in spirits and angels' (Mould 1951: 475).

12. For a classic study of Philo's theology, see Goodenough (1935).

Levelers and Fifth Monarchists. Early Quakers shared this renewed apocalyptic fervor of seventeenth-century England, which imagined the return of Christ to punish evil kings, nobles and prelates and establish a reign of the saints over a renovated earth.[13]

In the eighteenth and nineteenth centuries, renewed apocalyptic hopes of radical Protestantism were tempered and transformed by progressive political movements, such as liberalism and socialism. There emerged a new version of prophetic hope that imagined a process of historical transformation that would begin with the birth of Enlightened critical consciousness, and grow through education, medicine, technology and democracy to a world gradually delivered of physical illness and poverty to a just and happy future society. Human life would be greatly lengthened, and humans could enjoy the hundred years of blessed life of earlier Hebrew dreams, although still within an ultimately mortal world.[14]

As we have seen in Chapter 4, nineteenth-century feminism embraced this renewed vision of this-worldly progressive hope. Christian theology also was greatly influenced by the vision of progress. Immanuel Kant, in his classic work *Religion within the Limits of Reason Alone*, identified progress in reason and social justice as the true meaning of the Christian hope for the coming Kingdom of God.[15] Christian socialist theologians, such as Walter Rauschenbusch, at the end of the nineteenth century, taught a generation of American Christian ministers to identify the gospel with hope for progress in democracy and social justice and to shape their church ministries accordingly.[16]

Although this identification of the reign of God with social progress seemed to have died in Western Europe on the battlefields of the First World War, to be given the *coup de grâce* in the Neo-Orthodox theology of Karl Barth, this vision was not stifled altogether. In Latin American liberation theology it would be rediscovered and redeveloped in a Third World revolutionary form in the late 1960s. Twentieth-century feminist theology was also born in the 1960s in dialogue with these First and Third World liberation movements and their revived hope for the coming of a time of justice and peace on earth.

---

13. See Ruether 1992: 74-77; also Frend 1985; Cohn 1961; Reeves 1976; Hill 1975.

14. See Ruether 1970: esp. chs. 3-5.

15. Kant 1960: 113-14.

16. Rauschenbusch 1918.

Feminism, Future Hope and Eschatology

Both the ancient visions of personal immortality based on escape from the body and the earth and the modern vision of this-worldly progressive hope contain ambivalent views of women. Both these visions were shaped by male thinkers at the expense of women. In Plato's vision of the fall of the soul and its incarnation into the body, the soul is seen as normatively male. By extension its fullest and best expression is found in the noble Greek male.

In his *Timaeus* Plato asserts that if the soul lives justly, controlling the passions of the body, it will return at death to its native star. But if it fails to do so, it will be reincarnated into a woman and then into some animal 'which resembles the low estate into which it has fallen'. Only through successive reincarnations may the soul work its way back into the highest human form, the ruling class Greek male, and, by living well, escape the cycle of reincarnation.[17] Thus femaleness is linked with the body and its passions in a way incompatible with redemption from the body.

Although Christianity rejected the Platonic concept of reincarnation, it also tended to assume that the female nature was closer to sin, carnality and death than the male. Indeed women through their disobedience brought about the fall into sin and death in the first place. In the new dispensation in Christ, redemption has been extended to them, but in a way that negates their specific female nature. The 'good news' that in Christ 'there is no more male and female', was shaped by an androcentric anthropology in which the 'problem' of gender difference fell disproportionately on women. To become 'one in Christ', women must rise above both their sinful and their female natures, to become 'spiritually male'.[18]

Radical Christians through the centuries have interpreted this 'good news' for women as one that liberates women from subjugation to the male into a new autonomous personhood through renunciation of sex and childbearing, but mainline Catholic and Protestant Christianity strove to correct this radical view. Instead women were told they were saved by Christ only by redoubling their subjugation to the male as their 'head', whether that meant their husbands as wives or their male eccle-

17. Plato, *Timaeus* 49-50.
18. For the androcentric character of this text in Paul, see Fatum (1991).

siastic superiors as celibate 'sisters'. Thus redemption for women has been filtered through a deeply misogynist lens that identified femaleness with the sources of evil, that is, sex, sin and death, and the mortality of the body and the earth.

Modern progressive political thought, liberalism and socialism, and its male Christian theological expressions in the social gospel and liberation theology, likewise have exhibited their tendencies to shape their visions of redemption in ways that marginalize women. Both French and American revolutionary liberalism identified that 'equality' in which 'all men' are created in terms of reason and moral will. They assumed that these capacities predominated in free white propertied males and were lacking in women (also non-whites and slaves).

Not only were women excluded from the political rights of the new concept of the 'citizen' under the French and American revolutionary governments, but the subordination of all women was systematized. The exceptions in which unmarried or widowed women of property exercised political rights were deleted, making gender a systematic exclusion of all women as women from the rights of the citizen.[19] It would take a century and a half for this disparity to be overcome and women accorded the rights of 'the man and the citizen'. Even today remnants of the view that only males are public political persons who exercise full civil rights lingers in modern societies.

Socialism began with the claim that women would be liberated from domestic servitude by joining the workers' struggle. But Marxism soon interpreted this to mean that issues of gender per se were marginal and unimportant. Feminist movements that focused on liberating women from gender discrimination were 'bourgeois' and reactionary. The revolutionary socialist woman was to identify with the class struggle in a way that negated specifically female issues.[20] Latin American liberation theology has tended to follow the same bias, exalting the class struggle in a way that marginalizes, ignores or negates any specific focus on gender discrimination in society and even more in the church.[21]

19. Some women of property voted in the colonies, but all women as women were denied the right to vote under the American Constitution prior to the twenty-first amendment: see, for example, the political activity of Margaret Brent in the colony of Maryland; Ruether 1995c: 20-21, 35-36.

20. For the ambivalence of socialism toward women, see Rowbotham (1972: esp. Chapters 3–4).

21. Elsa Tamez, Mexican feminist theologian, sought to make Latin American

Feminist liberation theologies have responded to this misogynist bias in liberalism and socialism by adding women and gender issues into their visions of democratic political reform and revolutionary economic reconstruction. Patriarchy has been defined as the root problem of injustice. Social justice means overcoming it in all its aspects. Feminist theology has appropriated the symbol of the Kingdom (Reign or Kindom[22]) of God to represent that fulfillment of hope for a good society that will come about when women and men live in complete mutuality.

One Latin American feminist theologian, Brazilian Ivone Gebara, has raised questions about the continued attachment of liberation theology (and, by implication, feminist theology) to this biblical myth of a future time of complete and absolute conquest of all evil as the goal of their struggle for liberation. For Gebara this also means that feminist liberation theologians should abandon the corresponding myth of an original paradise prior to a fall into sin and death in which life on earth was in perfect harmony.[23]

Gebara questions the literalism of any belief in a 'perfect time' both 'once-upon-a-time' and in some future culmination of history. She also suggests that these absolute once and future points of reference in theology create a dualism between past and future good and present evil. This dualism lends itself to strategies of revolutionary violence, to which those in power respond with redoubled reactionary violence. Thus the myth of an original past and a final future of perfection feeds into a endless cycle of violence that continues to engulf Latin America and the world in the name of a redemptive struggle for justice.

Gebara also believes there has been a kind of 'fall' within human history that needs to be overcome, but it has been a more partial and relative 'fall'. She wishes to distinguish between the problems of life and death, joy and tragedy, which are the 'natural' and unchangeable conditions of finitude, and the construction of a system of domination that turns most humans and the earth into victims, even as some humans

---

liberation theologians respond to the women's issues in her book *Against Machismo: Interviews* (1987); see also Rosemary Ruether on the resistance of Gustavo Gutierrez to gender issues (Ruether 1996b: 28).

22. Feminists have sought to avoid the male and monarchical implications of the word 'kingdom' by using the more neutral 'reign of God'. Some have coined the term 'kindom' as a sound-alike but egalitarian term. See, for example, Isasi-Diaz (1996: 89 and 103 n. 8).

23. See Gebara 1995: 39-52, 71-88.

aggrandize power and wealth at the expense of these others.

Gebara suggests a psychological root of this construction of dominating power by males at the expense of women. The finitude of life, with its cycles of growth and decline, represented by the woman's womb pregnant with new life that may bring death to the mother in giving birth or a sickly child that soon dies, are experiences of life in the midst of fragility that are terrifying. Men have seen women as representatives of these frightening mysteries of birth and death, and project their own fears of vulnerability onto them.

By constructing systems of domination in which they see themselves as owning the birth process by owning women's bodies, then also owning the bodies of enslaved workers, of animals, of the earth itself, men seek to distance themselves from these fragilities of life, while securing for themselves invulnerable power over them. Thus any effort to create more just societies that share benefits equally with women and other victimized people not only threatens the advantages that rich and powerful males gain through domination, but opens up an abyss of fear that men will become subject to the same uncontrollable vicissitudes as women.

Gebara suggests that in order to create more just and mutual societies of men and women, and more sustainable relations with the earth, we need to do more than 'overthrow' political systems. We need to reconstruct our psychological culture and world view. We need to accept the finitude and partiality of mortal life in which joys are experienced in the midst of tragedies. The powerful male needs to be able to accept the same vulnerabilities as the female, and victims cease to dream of an escape into deathless perfection. Only then can we dismantle the systems that incarnate unjust domination of some at the expense of others, and live in mutual sharing of the fleeting but precious goods of life on a beautiful but fragile earth.

If Gebara has cast a skeptical eye on the myths of paradise and the Kingdom of God as points of reference for historical hope, what of the hope for immortality, for an escape of the soul from the 'corruptible body' into eternal life in a heavenly realm? Is this not a second form of escape from vulnerability in which humans have sought to deny their own finitude? Has perhaps the cultivation of hope for escape from death into immortal life been a key source of our disregard of our bodies, the earth and its creatures bound to the life cycles of birth, growth, decay and death? By imagining that some inner core of our personhood is immune to this life cycle, we deny our participation in it and imagine that we can freely toss our waste into it without affecting the basis of our own lives.[24]

An ecological spirituality demands that we accept that we too are fully of the earth, earthly. This means coming to terms with our mortality. We will not overcome our patterns of turning the waste side of our production and consumption life cycle into poisons until we learn to accept that we too are a part of the life cycle of the earth itself. This means learning to integrate our human processes into the natural processes that renew the earth, even as a forest uses every plant and animal body that dies and falls to the ground as part of a process of disintegration that is reintegrated as food and fertilizer for new growth.

We need to visualize ourselves as an integral part of a dynamic matrix of matter-energy in a continual process of conversion and transformation. This dynamic conversion of the matter-energy continuum has been in continual creativity since the explosion of the primal nucleus 18 billion years ago. Out of that continual reshaping of matter-energy the earth itself was formed and gave birth to the processes by which organic beings of ever greater complexity and capacity for consciousness developed.

Although humans are the apex, up to now, of this process of increasingly complex and conscious organic beings, we, as much as plants and other animals, are finite centers of life who exist for a season. When we die all the cells of our bodies disintegrate into the matrix of matter-energy to rise again in new forms, as part of a worm or a bird, a flower or a human. The matter of our bodies lives on in plants, animals and soil, even as our own living bodies are composed of substances that once were part of rocks, plants and animals, stretching back to prehistoric ferns and reptiles, before that to ancient biota that floated on the first seas of earth, and before that to the stardust of exploding galaxies.

The spirituality of recycling, integrating our life processes with that of the rest of the earth that sustains us, demands a deep conversion of consciousness. We have to accept our mortality and transience, relinquishing the illusion of permanent immortal selves that are exempt from this process. While this is a terrible word for those who see the individual self as ultimate, it can become a joyful word once we relax into knowing ourselves as an integral part of a Great Matrix of Being, that is ever

24. This ecofeminist critique of the quest for immortality is developed especially in Ruether (1995d).

renewing life in new creative forms out of the very processes of death. One generation of earth creatures die and disintegrate into the earth so another may arise from its womb. This is the real and only resurrection of the dead. As we surrender our ego-clinging to personal immortality, we find ourselves upheld by the immortality of the wondrous whole, 'in whom we live and move and have our being'.

Are these critiques of hope for future historical and otherworldly escape from finitude the end of any idea of redemption? Have such feminist critique simply ended all human hopes for a 'better world' on this earth? I think this does not mean a rejection of hope, but rather a focus on more authentic and possible hopes: hopes within the possibilities of finite life on earth. Such modest and earthly hopes are expressed in the Women's Creed written in preparation for the Fourth International Women's Conference in Bejing, China in September 1995. This creed names future hope as:

> Bread. A clean sky. Active peace. A woman's voice singing somewhere. The army disbanded. The harvest abundant. The wound healed. The child wanted. The prisoner freed. The body's integrity honored. The lover returned... Labor equal, fair and valued. No hand raised in any gesture but greeting. Secure interiors—of heart, home and land—so firm as to make secure borders irrelevant at last.[25]

These indeed are redemptive hopes enough for all of us.

25. This women's creed was sent to me courtesy of Catherine Keller of Drew Theological School in Madison, New Jersey; it was originally written by Robin Morgan for the Beijing Conference.

Bibliography

Adair, M.
    1992   'Will the Real Men's Movement Please Stand Up', in Hagan (1992: 63-66).

Amoah, E.
    1990   'Femaleness: Akan Concepts and Practices', in J. Becker, *Women, Religion and Sexuality: The Impact of Religious Teachings on Women* (Geneva: World Council of Churches): 129-53.

Astell, M.
    1970   *A Serious Proposal to the Ladies* (New York: Source Book [1701]).

Atkinson, J. (ed.)
    1966   *Luther's Works* (Philadephia: Fortress Press).

Bacon, M.H.
    1980   *Valiant Friend: The Life of Lucretia Mott* (New York: Walker).

Baird, J.L., and R.K. Ehrman
    1994   *The Letters of Hildegard of Bingen* (New York: Oxford University Press).

Barker, P.D.
    1995   'Caritas Pirckheimer: A Female Humanist Confronts the Reformation', *Sixteenth Century Journal* 26.2: 259-72.

Bene, C. (ed.)
    1990   *De Nobilitate et prescellentia forminei Sexus* (Geneva: Droz).

Bird, P.
    1981   'Male and Female he Created Them: Gen. 1:27b in the Context of the Priestly Account of Creation', *Harvard Theological Review* 74.2: 129-59.

Børresen, K.
    1995a   *Subordination and Equivalence: The Nature and Role of Woman in Augustine and Thomas Aquinas* (Kampen: Kok).
    1995b   'Julian of Norwich: A Model of Feminist Theology', in Børresen and Vogt 1995: 295-314.

Børreson, K. (ed.)
    1991   *Image of God and Gender Models* (Oslo: Solum Forlag).

Børresen, K., and K. Vogt (eds.)
    1995   *Women's Studies of the Christian and Islamic Traditions* (London: Kluwer Academic Publishers).

Boswell, J.
    1980   *Christianity, Social Tolerance and Homosexuality* (Chicago: Chicago University Press).

Brown, J.C., and C.R. Bohn (eds.)
    1989   *Christianity, Patriarchy and Abuse: A Feminist Critique* (New York: Pilgrim Press).

Burns, J. P.
    1981   *Theological Anthropology* (Philadelphia: Fortress Press).

Butterworth, G.W. (ed.)
    1966   *On First Principles* (New York: Harper & Row).

Cameron, R.D.
    1982   *The Other Gospels: Non-Canonical Gospel Texts* (Philadelphia: Westminster Press).

Cary, M.
    1647   'A Word in Season to the Kingdom of England', Thomason Tracts microfilms.
    1651   'The Little Horns Doom: A New and More Exact Mappe of New Jerusalem's Glory'.

Ceplair, L.
    1989   *The Public Years of Sarah and Angelina Grimké: Selected Writings, 1835–1839* (New York: Columbia University Press).

Chaucer, G.
    1932   *The Complete Poetical Works of Geoffrey Chaucer* (New York: Macmillan).

Clark, E.E.
    1979   *John Chrysostom and Friends* (Lewiston, NY: Edwin Mellen Press).

Cloke, G.
    1995   *This Female Man of God: Women and Spiritual Power in the Patristic Age, AD 350–450* (London: Routledge).

Cohn, N.
    1961   *The Pursuit of the Millenium: Revolutionary Messianism in Medieval and Reformation Europe* (New York: Harper & Row).

Colledge, E., and J. Walsh (eds.)
    1978   *The Book of Showings to the Anchoress Julian of Norwich* (Toronto: Pontifical Institute of Medieval Studies).

Connelly, H.
    1916   *The So-Called Egyptian Church Order and Related Documents* (Cambridge: Cambridge University Press).

Crossan, D.
    1991   *The Historical Jesus: The Life of a Mediterranean Jewish Peasant* (San Francisco: HarperSanFrancisco).

Cumont, F.
    1912   *Astrology and Religion among the Greeks and Romans* (New York: Dover).

D'Angelo, M.R.
    1995   'Veils, Virgins and Tongues of Men and Angels: Women's Heads in Early Christianity', in H. Eilberg-Schwartz and W. Doniger (eds.), *Off with her Head: The Denial of Women's Identity in Myth, Religion and Culture* (Berkeley, CA: University of California Press): 131-64.

Davies, S.
1980   *The Revolt of the Widows: The Social World of the Apocryphal Acts* (Carbon-dale, IL: Southern Illinois University Press).

Dodd, C.H.
1963   *The Interpretation of the Fourth Gospel* (New York: Cambridge University Press).

Douglass, J.
1974   'Women and the Continental Reformation', in Ruether (1974: 309-14).

Eckerstein, L.
1896   *Women under Monasticism* (Cambridge: Cambridge University Press).

Ellis, M.H.
1990   *Beyond Innocence and Redemption: Confronting the Holocaust and Israeli Power: Creating a Moral Future for the Jewish People* (San Francisco: Harper & Row).

1994   *Ending Auschwitz: The Future of Jewish and Christian Cultural Life* (Louisville, KY: Westminster/John Knox Press).

Engel, M.P.
1992   'Historical Theology and Violence against Women: Unearthing a Popular Tradition of Just Battery', in M.P. Engel and W.E. Wyman, *Revisioning the Past: Prospects in Historical Theology* (Philadelphia: Fortress Press): 51-76.

Fabella, V.
1993   *Beyond Bonding: A Third World Women's Theological Journey* (Manila: Institute of Women's Studies).

Fatum, L.
1991   'Image of God and Glory of Man', in Børreson (1991: 56-137).

Fell, M.
1989   *Women's Speaking Justified and other Seventeenth Century Quaker Writings about Women* (ed. C. Trevett; London: Quaker Home Service).

Ferguson, M.
1985   *First Feminists: British Women Writers, 1578–1799* (Bloomington, IL: Indiana University Press).

Findon, C.
1995   *Moments with God: The Battered Woman's Relationship with God and her Journey as she Moves Beyond the Abuse* (DMin thesis, Garrett-Evangelical Theological Seminary, June).

Finson, S.D.
1991   *Women and Religion: A Bibliographic Guide to Christian Feminist Liberation Theology* (Toronto: University of Toronto Press).

Franklin, J.C.
1978   *Mystical Transformations: The Imagery of Liquids in Mechtild of Magdeburg* (London: Association of University Presses).

Frend, W.H.C.
1985   *The Donatist Church: A Movement of Protest in Roman North Africa* (Oxford: Clarendon Press).

Gebara, I.
1995   *Teología a Ritmo de Mujer* (Madrid: San Pablo).

Glatzer, N.
1971   *The Essential Philo* (New York: Schocken Books).

Goldstein, V.S.
    1960   'The Human Situation: A Feminine View', *Journal of Religion* 40: 100-12.

Goodenough, E.
    1935   *By Light, Light: The Mystic Gospel of Hellenistic Judaism* (New Haven, CT: Yale University Press).
    1968   *The Theology of Justin Martyr* (Amsterdam: Philo Press).

Gouge, W.
    1622   *Of Domesticall Duties* (London).

Green, D. (ed.)
    1980   *Lucretia Mott: Her Complete Speeches and Sermons* (Lewiston, NY: Edwin Mellen Press).

Grey, M.
    1989   *Redeeming the Dream: Feminism, Redemption and Christian Tradition* (London: SPCK).

Gross, R.
    1993   *Buddhism after Patriarchy: A Feminist History, Analysis and Reconstruction of Buddhism* (Albany, NY: SUNY Press).

Hagan, K.L. (ed.)
    1992   *Women Respond to the Men's Movement: A Feminist Collection* (San Francisco: Harper & Row).

Halkes, C.
    1989   *New Creation: Christian Feminism and the Renewal of the Earth* (London: SPCK).

Hart, C., and J. Bishop (eds.)
    1990   *Scivias* (New York: Paulist Press).

Hassan, R.
    1987   'Man–Woman Equality in the Islamic Tradition', *Harvard Divinity School Bulletin* 17.2: 2-4.

Henderson, K.U., and B.F. McManus
    1985   *Half-Humankind: Contexts and Texts of the Controversy about Women in England, 1540–1640* (Urbana, IL: Illinois University Press).

Herlihy, D.
    1990   *Opera Mulieribus: Women and Work in Medieval Europe* (New York: McGraw–Hill).

Heyward, C.
    1982   *The Redemption of God* (Lanham, MD: University Press of America).
    1989   *Touching our Strength: The Erotic as Power and the Love of God* (San Francisco: Harper & Row).

Hill, C.
    1975   *The World Turned Upside Down: Radical Ideas During the English Revolution* (New York: Viking).

Hoffmann, R.J.
    1984   *Marcion: On the Restitution of Christianity: An Essay on the Development of Radical Paulinist Theology in the Second Century* (Chico, CA: Scholars Press).

Hopkins, L.
    1991   *Women Who Would Be Kings: Female Rulers of the Sixteenth Century* (New York: St Martin's Press).

Inclusive Language Lectionary Committee
 1983 *An Inclusive Language Lectionary: Readings for Year A* (Philadelphia: West-
    minster Press).
Irwin, J.L.
 1979 *Womanhood in Radical Protestantism, 1525–1675* (Lewiston, NY: Edwin
    Mellen Press).
Isasi-Diaz, A.M.
 1996 *Mujerista Theology* (Maryknoll, NY: Orbis Books).
Isherwood, L., and D. McEwan
 1993 *Introducing Feminist Theology* (Sheffield: Sheffield Academic Press).
Jenkins, C. (ed.)
 1907/1908 *Journal of Theological Studies* 9: 500-14.
Jonas, H.
 1963 *The Gnostic Religion: The Message of the Alien God and the Beginnings of
    Christianity* (Boston: Beacon Press).
Kadel, A.
 1995 *Matrology: A Bibliography of Writings by Christian Women from the First to the
    Fifteenth Centuries* (New York: Continuum).
Kant, E.
 1960 *Religion within the Limits of Reason Alone (1793)* (New York: Harper &
    Brothers).
King, J. (ed.)
 1847 *Commentaries on the Book of Genesis* (Edinburgh: Calvin Translation Soci-
    ety).
Knox, J.
 1985 *The Political Writings of John Knox: The First Blast of the Trumpet against the
    Monstrous Regiment of Women and Other Selected Writings* (Introduction by
    M.A. Breslow; London: Associated University Presses).
Kraemer, R.S.
 1988 *Maenads, Martyrs, Matrons and Monastics: A Sourcebook on Women's Religions
    in the Greco-Roman World* (Philadelphia: Fortress Press).
Kraft, R.A.
 1965 *The Apostolic Fathers: Translation and Commentary* (New York: Thomas
    Nelson).
Kyung, C.H.
 1990a *Struggle to Be the Sun Again: Introducing Asian Women's Theology*
    (Maryknoll, NY: Orbis Press).
 1990b 'Han-pu-ri: Doing Theology from a Korean Woman's Perspective', in
    V. Fabella and S.A. Lee-Park (eds.), *We Dare to Dream: Doing Theology as
    Asian Women* (Maryknoll, NY: Orbis Press): 134-46.
Laeuchli, S.
 1972 *Power and Sexuality: The Emergence of Canon Law at the Council of Elvira*
    (Philadelphia: Temple University Press).
Layton, B. (ed.)
 1980 *The Rediscovery of Gnosticism. I. The School of Valentinus* (Leiden: E.J. Brill).
Lerner, G.
 1967 *The Grimké Sisters from South Carolina: Rebels against Slavery* (Boston:
    Houghton Mifflin).

MacDonald, D.R.

    1983   *The Legend and the Apostle: The Battle for Paul in Story and Canon* (Phila-delphia: Westminster Press).

    1987   *There Is No Male and Female* (Philadelphia: Fortress Press).

Mack, P.

    1992   *Visionary Women: Ecstatic Prophecy in Seventeenth Century England* (Berkeley, CA: University of California Press).

McNeil, J.T. (ed.)

    1960   *Institutes of the Christian Religion* (Philadelphia: Westminster Press).

Meeks, W.

    1983   *The First Urban Christians: The Social World of the Apostle Paul* (New Haven, CT: Yale University Press).

Mendelson, I.

    1955   *Religions of the Ancient Near East: Sumero-Akkadian Religious Texts and Ugaritic Epics* (New York: Liberal Arts Press).

Miller, R.J.

    1994   *The Complete Gospels* (Sonoma, CA: Polebridge Press).

Mould, E.W.K.

    1951   *Essentials of Bible History* (New York: Ronald Press).

Mowinckel, S.

    1955   *He that Cometh: The Messiah Concept in the Old Testament and Later Judaism* (Nashville, TN: Abingdon Press).

Newman, B.

    1987   *Sister of Wisdom: St Hildegard's Theology of the Feminine* (Berkeley, CA: University of California).

    1995   *From Virile Woman to WomanChrist: Studies in Medieval Religion and Litera-ture* (Philadelphia: University of Philadelphia Press).

Nicolson, L. (ed.)

    1990   *Feminism/Post-Modernism* (New York: Routledge).

Nyssa, G.

    1967   *Ascetical Works, Fathers of the Church* (Washington, DC: Catholic Univer-sity Press of America), vol. V.

Oduyoye, M.A.

    1992   'Women and Ritual in Africa', in M.A. Oduyoye and M. Kanyoro (eds.), *The Will to Arise: Women, Tradition and the Church in Africa* (Maryknoll, NY: Orbis Press).

    1995   *Daughters of Anowa: African Women and Patriarchy* (Maryknoll: NY: Orbis Press).

Oduyoye, M.A., and E. Amoah

    1988   'The Christ for African Women', in V. Fabella and M.A. Oduyoye (eds.), *With Passion and Compassion: Third Women Doing Theology* (Maryknoll, NY: Orbis Press): 35-36.

Pagels, E.

    1979   *The Gnostic Gospels* (New York: Random House).

Park, A.S.

    1993   *The Wounded Heart of God: The Asian Concept of Han and the Christian Doctrine of Sin* (Nashville, TN: Abingdon Press).

Perkins, W.
    1590   *Christian Oeconomie* (London).
    1970   *The Works of William Perkins* (Appleford: Sutton Courtenay Press).
Perry, R.
    1986   *The Celebrated Mary Astell: An Early English Feminist* (Chicago, IL: University of Chicago Press).
Phipps, W.
    1970   *Was Jesus Married?* (New York: Harper & Row).
Plaskow, J.
    1980   *Sex, Sin and Grace: Women's Experience and the Theologies of Reinhold Niebuhr and Paul Tillich* (Lanham, MD: University Press of America).
    1990   *Standing again at Sinai: Judaism from a Feminist Perspective* (San Francisco: Harper & Row).
Pomeroy, S.B.
    1975   *Goddesses, Whores, Wives and Slaves: Women in Classical Antiquity* (New York: Schocken Books).
    1984   *Women in Hellenistic Egypt: From Alexander to Cleopatra* (New York: Schocken Books).
Pringle, W. (ed.)
    1856   *Commentaries on the Epistles to Timothy, Titus and Philemon* (Edinburgh: Calvin Translation Society).
Prusak, B.P.
    1974   'Women: Seductive Siren and Source of Sin?', in Ruether (1974: 89-116).
Reeves, M.
    1976   *Joachim of Fiore and the Prophetic Future* (San Francisco: Harper & Row).
Roberts, A., and J. Donaldson (eds.)
    1870   *Acts of Paul, Ante-Nicene Fathers*, XVI (New York: Charles Scribner's Sons).
Robinson, J. (ed.)
    1977   *The Nag Hammadi Library in English* (New York: Harper & Row).
Robinson, J.M.
    1975   'Jesus as Sophos and Sophia: Wisdom Tradition and the Gospels', in Wilkin (1975): 1-16.
Rowbotham, S.
    1972   *Women, Resistance and Revolution* (New York: Random House).
Ruether, R.R.
    1970   *The Radical Kingdom: The Western Experience of Messianic Hope* (New York: Paulist Press).
    1974a   'Misogynism and Virginal Feminism in the Fathers of the Church', in Ruether 1974: 153-55.
    1974b   *Faith and Fratricide: The Theological Roots of Anti-Semitism* (New York: Seabury Press).
    1979a   'Mothers of the Church: Ascetic Women in the Late Patristic Age', in Ruether and McLaughlin 1979: 71-98.
    1979b   *Mary: The Feminine Face of the Church* (London: SCM Press).
    1981   'Women in Utopian Movements', in R. Ruether and R. Keller, *Women and Religion in America: The Nineteenth Century* (New York: Harper & Row): 46-100.

1983	*Sexism and God-Talk: Toward a Feminist Theology* (London: SCM Press).
1990	'Prophets and Humanists: Types of Religious Feminism in Stuart England', *Journal of Religion* 70.1.
1992	*Gaia and God: An Ecofeminist Theology of Earth Healing* (San Francisco: Harper & Row).
1993	'Can Christology Be Liberated from Patriarchy?', in Stevens 1993: 7-29.
1994	'Christianity and Women in the Modern World', in A. Sharma (ed.) *Today's Woman in World Religion* (Albany, NY: SUNY Press): 267-302.
1995a	'Feminist Metanoia and Soul-Making', in J. Ochshorn and E. Cole (eds.), *Women's Spirituality, Women's Lives* (New York: Haworth Press): 33-44.
1995b	'Witches and Jews: The Demonic Alien in Christian Culture', in *New Woman, New Earth: Sexist Ideologies and Human Liberation* (repr. with new preface; Boston: Beacon [1975]).
1995c	'Catholic Women in North America', in R.S. Keller and R.R. Ruether (eds.), *In Our Own Voices: Four Centuries of American Women's Religious Writings* (San Francisco: Harper & Row): 20-36.
1995d	'The Cycle of Life and Death in Ecofeminist Spirituality', *Creation Spirituality* 11.2: 35-38.
1996a	'Fight for Women's Vote, Nation's Identity', *National Catholic Reporter*, 15 November.
1996b	'Rift between Gutiérrez and Peru Women', *National Catholic Reporter*, 18 October.
1998	*Gender and Redemption: A Historical Theology* (Philadelphia: Fortress Press).

Ruether, R.R. (ed.)

1974	*Religion and Sexism: Images of Women in the Jewish and Christian Traditions* (New York: Simon & Schuster).

Ruether, R.R., and E. McLaughlin (eds.)

1979	*Women of Spirit: Female Leadership in the Jewish and Christian Traditions* (New York: Simon & Schuster).

Ruether, R.R., and H.J. Ruether

1989	*The Wrath of Jonah: The Crisis of Religious Nationalism in the Israeli-Palestinian Conflict* (San Francisco: Harper & Row).

Sands, K.

1994	*Escape from Paradise: Evil and Tragedy in Feminist Theology* (Philadelphia: Fortress Press).

Schaberg, J.

1987	*The Illegitimacy of Jesus* (San Francisco: Harper & Row).

Schneir, M. (ed.)

1972	*Feminism: The Essential Historical Writings* (New York: Vintage Books).

Schillebeeckx, E.

1979	*Jesus: An Experiment in Christology* (New York: Seabury).

Schüssler Fiorenza, E.

1975	'Wisdom Mythology and the Christological Hymns of the New Testament', in Wilkin (1975): 17-42.
1979	'Word, Spirit and Power: Women in Early Christian Communities', in Ruether and McLaughlin (1979): 39-44.

Schüssler Fiorenza, F.
    1983   *In Memory of Her: A Feminist Theological Reconstruction of Christian Origins* (New York: Crossroad).
    1987   'Redemption', *The New Dictionary of Theology* (Wilmington, DE: Michael Glazier).
Shema, R.
    1997   *The Reenvisioning of Shakta-Tantra as a Foundation for a Hindu Ecofeminist Philosophy* (MA thesis, Claremont Graduate School, Claremont, CA, June).
Sherfey, M.J.
    1972   *The Nature and Evolution of Female Sexuality* (New York: Random House).
Shiva, V.
    1988   *Staying Alive: Women, Ecology and Survival in India* (Delhi: Kali for Women).
Smith, H.L.
    1982   *Reason's Disciples: Seventeenth Century English Feminists* (Chicago, IL: University of Illinois Press).
Smith, P.
    1920   *The Age of the Reformation* (New York: Henry Holt).
Soelle, D.
    1975   *Suffering* (Philadelphia: Fortress Press).
    1990   *Window of Vulnerability: A Political Spirituality* (Philadelphia: Fortress Press).
    1995a   *Theology for Skeptics: Reflections on God* (Philadelphia: Fortress Press).
    1995b   *Creative Disobedience* (Cleveland, OH: Pilgrim Press).
Speizman, M.D., and J.C. Kronich (eds.)
    1975   'A Seventeenth Century Quaker Women's Declaration', *Signs: Journal of Women in Culture and Society* 1.1: 231-45.
Spreght, R.
    1617   *A Mousell for Melastomus, The Cynicall Bayter of and foule-mouthed Barker against Evahs Sex* (N. Oakes for T. Archer).
Stevens, M. (ed.)
    1993   *Reconstructing the Christ Symbol: Essays in Feminist Christology* (New York: Paulist Press).
Swidler, L.
    1979   *Biblical Affirmations of Women* (Philadelphia: Westminster Press).
Tamez, E.
    1987   *Against Machismo: Interviews* (Oak Park, IL: Meyer-Stone Books).
    1992   *Quetzacoatl y el Dios Christiano, Quadernos de Teología y Cultura*, 6 (San José, Costa Rica).
Teske, R.J. (ed.)
    1991   *The Fathers of the Church* (Washington, DC: Catholic University Press of America), vol. LXXXIV.
Thompson, J.L.
    1988   '*Creata Ad Imaginem Dei, Licet Secundo Gradu*: Women as the Image of God according to John Calvin', *Harvard Theological Review* 81.2: 125-43.
Trevett, C.
    1996   *Montanism: Gender, Authority and the New Prophecy* (Cambridge: Cambridge University Press).

von Campenhausen, H.
    1963   *The Fathers of the Church* (London: A. & C. Black).
von Magdeburg, M.
    1991   *The Flowing Light of Divinity* (ed. C. Mesch Galvani; New York: Garland Press).
Wallis Budge, E.A.
    1961   *Osiris: Egyptian Religion of Resurrection* (New York: University Books).
Weisner, M.E.
    1986   *Working Women in Renaissance Germany* (New Brunswick, NJ: Rutgers University Press).
    1988   'Women's Response to the Reformation', in R.P.-C. Hsia, *The German People and the Reformation* (Ithaca, NY: Cornell University Press): 148-71.
    1993   *Women and Gender in Early Modern Europe* (Cambridge: Cambridge University Press).
Welter, B.
    1976   *Dimity Convictions: The American Woman in the Nineteenth Century* (Athens, OH: Ohio University Press).
Wemple, S.
    1983   *Women in Frankish Society: Marriage and the Cloister, 500–900 AD* (Philadelphia: Pennsylvania University Press).
West, E.W.
    1965   *The Sacred Books of the East: Pahlavi Texts* (repr.; Delhi: Mortilal Banarsidass [1897]), V.
White, A., and L.S. Taylor
    1904   *Shakerism: Its Meaning and Message* (Columbia, OH: Frederick J. Heer Press).
Wilkin, R.L. (ed.)
    1975   *Aspects of Wisdom in Judaism and Early Christianity* (South Bend, IN: Notre Dame Press).
Williams, D.
    1991   'Black Women's Surrogacy Experience and the Christian Notion of Redemption', in P.M. Cooey, W.R. Eakins and J.B. McDaniel (eds.), *After Patriarchy: Feminist Transformation of the World Religions* (Maryknoll, NY: Orbis Press): 1-14.
    1993a   'A Womanist Perspective on Sin', in E. Townes (ed.), *A Troubling in My Soul: Womanist Perspectives on Evil* (Maryknoll, NY: Orbis Press): 130-49.
    1993b   *Sisters in the Wilderness: The Challenge of Womanist Godtalk* (Maryknoll, NY: Orbis Press).
Wire, A.
    1990   *The Corinthian Women Prophets: A Reconstruction through Paul's Rhetoric* (Philadelphia: Fortress Press).
Youngs, B.S., and C. Green (eds.)
    1856   *Testimony of Christ's Second Appearing* (Albany, NY: Van Benthysen).

INDEXES

INDEX OF REFERENCES

BIBLE

Index of Authors

Other Books in the Introductions in Feminist Theology Series

INTRODUCING ASIAN FEMINIST THEOLOGY
Kwok Pui-lan

This book introduces the history, critical issues, and direction of feminist theology as a grassroots movement in Asia. Kwok Pui-lan takes care to highlight the diversity of this broad movement, noting that not all women theologians in Asia embrace feminism. Amid a diverse range of sociopolitical, religiocultural, and postcolonial contexts, this book lifts up the diversity of voices and ways of doing feminist theology while attending to women's experiences, how the Bible is interpreted, and the ways that Asian religious traditions are appropriated. It searches out a passionate, life-affirming spirituality through feminine images of God, new metaphors for Christ, and reformulations of sin and redemption.
(Coming in fall 2000)

INTRODUCING THEALOGY: DISCOURSE ON THE GODDESS
Melissa Raphael

Introducing Thealogy provides an accessible but critical introduction to the relationship of religion, theo/alogy, and gender, especially as these concepts unfold in the revival of Goddess religion among feminists in Europe, North America, and Australasia. Raphael focuses on the boundaries of this broad movement, what is meant by the Goddess, thealogy in history and ethics, the political implications of the movement, and how it relates to feminist witchcraft.
0-8298-1379-9   Paper/184 pages/$17.95

INTRODUCING BODY THEOLOGY
Lisa Isherwood and Elizabeth Stuart

Because Christianity asserts that God was incarnated in human form, one might expect that its theologies would be body affirming. Yet for women (and indeed also for gay men) the body has been the site of oppression. *Introducing Body Theology* offers a body-centered theology that discusses cosmology, ecology, ethics, immortality, and sexuality, in a concise introduction that proposes and encourages a positive theology of the body.
0-8298-1375-6   Paper/168 pages/$16.95

INTRODUCING A PRACTICAL FEMINIST THEOLOGY OF WORSHIP
JANET WOOTTON

Only three great woman-songs are retained in the Bible: Deborah's song for ordinary people, Hannah's song of triumph, and Mary's song at meeting her cousin Elizabeth. Many others, such as Miriam's song, are truncated or overshadowed by male triumphs. *Introducing a Practical Feminist Theology of Worship* begins by revealing how women have been "whispering liturgy." It then explores female images of God, discusses how worship spaces function, and offers practical suggestions for how women can use words and movements to construct authentic forms of worship.
(Coming in fall 2000)

Other Books of Interest from The Pilgrim Press*

RE-IMAGINING THE DIVINE:
CONFRONTING THE BACKLASH AGAINST FEMINIST THEOLOGY
LAUREL C. SCHNEIDER

"With this bold, eloquent, and carefully reasoned book, Laurel Schneider challenges us to step outside the confines of monotheism and trinitarianism and take seriously the implications of the rich variety of religious experience. This book represents a significant innovation in constructive theology in general and in feminist theology, in particular, offering compelling insights for theorists and practitioners of feminist spirituality."
   —Sharon Welch, Professor of Religious Studies, University of Missouri, Columbia
0-8298-1289-X   Cloth/224 pages/$19.95

THE GREAT COMMANDMENT:
A THEOLOGY OF RESISTANCE AND TRANSFORMATION
ELEANOR H. HANEY

"Eleanor Haney is that rarity among white theologians, an activist scholar who lives in alliance with alienated secularists, low-income women, church members, indigenous people on Turtle Island, bankers, Siamese cats, and the feminist spiritual community. Her vision, deeply rooted in Christian traditions and formed in worship, has been shaped by such womanist theologians as Delores Williams and Emilie Townes. Her irenic spirit is both intellectually rigorous and mystical. She challenges our economic systems with the same vigor she uses to conceive Emmanuel as power in relationship. Never content merely with deconstruction, Haney here offers humans and other denizens of the earth a way of living with sustainability, justice, and well-being." —Susan E. Davies, coeditor of *Ending Racism in the Church*
0-8298-1245-8   Paper/152 pages/$12.95

To order call 1-800-537-3394, fax 216-736-3713,
or visit our Web site at www.pilgrimpress.com.
(Prices do not include shipping and handling.) Prices subject to change without notice.